Praise for *The Monks and Me*

"A magnificent book that eloquently juxtaposes Thich Nhat Hanh's Buddhist philosophy against modern day living—inspired, as seen through Paterson's eyes. This book is a revelation of spirituality in quotidian things, of balance and fragility in the midst of chaos, and most of all a testimony to mindfulness. It is a must read for anyone who wants simple recipes for ethical living. Paterson's exploration uncovers the bedrock for social development through personal excellence."
—Sema K. Sgaier, PhD,
Bill & Melinda Gates Foundation

"Alive with deep truths resounding loud and clear in the small, amazing moments of everyday life, Paterson reminds us of what's possible when we take the time to stop, look, and listen. An entertaining and juicy primer on the basic guidelines for a richer life."
—Ragini Michaels, author of *Unflappable*

"I enjoyed this book enormously. It reminded me in the most concrete terms what I already know but tend to forget: Take joy, have compassion, be patient, pay attention, let go, slow down. Wake up! Each little story—my favorite may be the one about the boy saving the ants—is a reminder to us all to be kind and be present."
—Margaret Hawkins, author of *A Year of Cats and Dogs* and *After Schizophrenia: The Story of My Sister's Reawakening after 30 Years*

The Monks and Me

The Monks and Me

How 40 Days in Thich Nhat Hanh's French
Monastery Guided Me Home

Mary Paterson

"In, out" poem reprinted from *The Heart of the Buddha's Teachings* by Thich Nhat Hanh (1998) with permission of Parallax Press, Berkeley, California, www.parallax.org.

Cover design by www.levanfisherdesign.com/Barbara Fisher
Interior by StanInfo

Hampton Roads Publishing Company, Inc.
Charlottesville, VA 22906
Distributed by Red Wheel/Weiser, LLC
www.redwheelweiser.com

Library of Congress Cataloging-in-Publication Data

Paterson, Mary, 1963-
The monks and me : what a bunch of singing Buddhists, a fat suitcase and a single pomegranate seed can show us about taking refuge in our wise selves/Mary Paterson.
    pages cm
    Includes bibliographical references and index.
    ISBN 978-1-57174-685-6 (alk. paper)

1. Paterson, Mary, 1963- 2. Spiritual biography--Canada. 3. Village des pruniers (Buddhist community) I. Title.
    BQ978.A753P38 2012
    294.3092--dc23
    [B]
                                      2012010852

ISBN: 978-1-57174-685-6

VG

10 9 8 7 6 5 4 3 2 1

For my mother and father, with love

Contents

Author's Note

Iwould like to take a moment to clarify that I have written about my forty-day pilgrimage to Plum Village based solely on my own observations and reflections, as I attempted to absorb and apply the teachings of the Venerable Thich Nhat Hanh, within his Buddhist monastery in France. My writings are not meant to be a scholarly examination of the teachings of the Buddha or those of Thich Nhat Hanh. And, importantly, my discoveries are in no way connected to Thich Nhat Hanh's specific counsel. For comprehensive insight into the vast and intricate teachings of the Buddha, I encourage you to explore the many exemplary books written by Thich Nhat Hanh.

All the names of the people within this book, including my fellow pilgrims, have been changed with the exception of the following people: my brothers, David and Iain, and my sister-in-law Janice. Also, Doug is really Doug. My fellow pilgrim, Stuart the Scot, is really a Scottish man named Stuart, and I might add that the Scot was delighted to appear in this book, even without knowing what I would say about him, trusting soul. And finally, the Sisters Pine, Prune, Hanh Nghiêm and An Nghiêm have all graciously granted their permission to be included as themselves.

The affectionate name for the Venerable Thich Nhat Hanh is Thây (pronounced "Tie"), which is Vietnamese for "teacher." I regularly use his affectionate name throughout this book.

And one more thing before we start: I want to express my deep thanks to you for entering into this journey with me. I have written *The Monks and Me* for you.

May you take refuge within your wise self and be guided Home. And may that bring you great joy.

Introduction
Leaving Home to Find *Home*

In the stormy ocean of life, take refuge in yourself.

—THICH NHAT HANH

My mother died many years ago. After her death, I found great healing through the Eastern teachings of yoga and meditation. But I also noticed something else. The more I practiced and applied these dynamic techniques, the more joy I felt, and the richer my experiences in the whole of my life. These masterful practices acted as a kind of life support for all my various difficulties and challenges, the ones that come with being human. But, here's the thing: even though yoga and meditation benefited me immensely, I didn't consistently apply these teachings in my life. And then my father died. And there it was. I felt I had nowhere to stand. I had lost the connection to my familiar inner Home.

Death can be a destabilizing force. And when it touches you closely, you must somehow discover a way to find and rebuild your secure Home. A forty-day pilgrimage is what I came up with. The longest meditation retreat I had ever undertaken had been ten days in length. Maybe forty days would bring me closer to the strength and love and Home I needed to reconstruct. Maybe a six-week pilgrimage with a wise monk at the helm would not only bring deeper healing from the deaths of my parents, but also serve as guidance throughout the turbulent waters of life. This ocean, as we all know, is sometimes calm and sometimes stormy. All of us need to be well-equipped for those stormy days.

In yogic science, cycles are often used to enhance life-affirming habits and advance one on the path of wisdom. A forty-day sacred journey supports the philosophy of the ancient yogis. Within many cultural and spiritual traditions, the span of forty days is recognized as a key interval in which the unfolding and recognition of truth happens. Christ prayed and fasted for forty days in the desert to prepare for and understand his purpose; so did the prophet Muhammad in a cave. Moses was transformed by this time on Mount Sinai. In the forty-day Christian season of Lent, followers give up a pleasure or vice. And the Buddha enjoyed the peace of enlightenment under the Boddhi tree for a period just exceeding forty days.

I was forty years old when my father died. Knowing that a forty-day spiritual practice has the power to be incredibly transformative, entering into this forty-day journey of renewal at this time would be to honor synchronicity. So, under a cold November sky, with the mystical number forty by my side, I crossed an ocean and set off for my pilgrimage. For six weeks I lived essentially as a nun, alongside the Sisters and Brothers of Plum Village, in their beloved Buddhist community in the Aquitaine countryside of France. During their monastic winter retreat, under the tutelage of world-renowned Vietnamese Zen master, author, peace and human rights activist, and Nobel Peace Prize nominee Thich Nhat Hanh, I meditated, gardened, walked, reflected on life, communed with pilgrims from all over the world, and looked my various demons straight in the eye as I listened intently to a wise eighty-four-year-old monk talk about the sacred and ancient teachings of the Buddha.

Each monastic winter retreat follows a theme that is announced on the first day. For this particular retreat, Thich Nhat Hanh chose to focus specifically on addressing the new world order, emphasizing the importance of *applying* the Buddha's teachings to our lives within the current times. This wise monk taught the necessity of *calling the suffering by its true name*, understanding that we are now faced with environmental destruction, fear, terrorism, emotional distress, fractured families, and a multitude of physical and mental illnesses. Through the Buddhist practice of *mindfulness*, of touching life deeply in every moment, compassion arises, wounds heal, and you become rooted in courage, strength, and wisdom. This is *taking refuge in the self*. Mindful awareness of the breath unites your body and mind, and this generates insight. You experience breakthroughs into the nature of reality, and you recognize your interconnection with all life. And then your strong, enlightened self can transform and heal all the beings of the world. You are not alone.

The American writer Annie Dillard said: "The impulse to keep to yourself what you have learned is not only shameful, it is destructive. Anything you do not give freely and abundantly becomes lost to you."

And so, with Dillard's motto in mind, here I am, writing about the forty days in a Vietnamese monastery in France that taught me how to take refuge within my wise self, and find Home.

Entering the Monastery

I am standing just outside a train station in the Aquitaine region of France. "There she is," I think. It's not
difficult to find my ride; she's the only woman here with
a shaved head and muddy brown monastic robes. I walk
toward her, and am immediately welcomed with a warm
smile. Sister An Nghiêm is a black American who formerly worked for the mayor in Washington, DC. And
here she is now, in a small village in the south of France,
driving me to her beloved Buddhist monastery.

Along for the ride are two other women—a warm
Brit who will stay at the monastery for one week, and an
icy American. After a forty-minute journey through the
stunning French countryside, we pull up to the main grey
stone building of New Hamlet, one of two residences for
nuns at Plum Village. Glorious, rolling moss-green hills
of just-finished purple grapevines and fields of towering sunflowers with heads the size of dinner plates that
only a month ago would have been in full golden bloom
surround several large, ancient-looking buildings. The
rustic, wooden sign on the main building reads HAMEAU
NOUVEAU, VILLAGE DES PRUNIERS. I am looking at my new
home for the next forty days.

I enter the majestic refurbished French farmhouse
and immediately feel relief. My shoulders plunge two full
inches, mercifully, as if a hefty load of worry has instantly
vanished into thin air. The front room of New Hamlet is
inviting and bright and brimming with shaved heads and

1

brown robes, all milling about, with the kind of gaiety one might not expect to find in an ascetic monastery. When I look out the back window, I see a massive brass gong hanging majestically in an open temple-like structure with four beams supporting a double-canopied roof, with curled edges like a blossoming lotus flower. The Asian-inspired building sits in an open field amongst rows of apple trees and grape vines. I haven't been here for more than five minutes when a joyous nun, a Vietnamese Sister with a stunningly sculpted face of golden hue, touches my elbow and says, "I am so happy to meet you." I can tell she means it. The nun has a beaming smile and mischievous manner about her. Later on, during dinner, I will become mesmerized while watching her eat—this Sister has the most powerful scalp muscles I have ever seen—more than all the other nuns here, and more than any bald-headed man I know. I will gaze in wonder as her head comes alive with pulsating ripples that would challenge the best muscle-bound wrestler.

After we exchange a few pleasantries, another friendly Sister leads me toward the back of the building, up some stairs, and down a long hallway to the bedrooms. My suitcase in tow, I now stand facing a sand-colored door, looking at a sign that says EAGLE. In Native Indian tradition, the eagle is considered to be the "messenger to the creator." This is because the eagle is a leader—the bird that flies the highest and sees the farthest. It is the one that carries your messages up to God. It is said that this majestic creature represents great power, courage, and vision.

I look at the door of the room next to mine. The sign hanging there says PEACE. That's nice, I think. But I'm happy to be sleeping with the bird that has the direct line to the Infinite.

My room is very basic. There is no closet and no bed-side table. There is barely space for the two tiny beds. This room is the smallest at New Hamlet, but luckily I will have this monastic abode all to myself. I hoist my heavy suitcase onto one of the cots, and have to bend down in order to peek out the window, an ancient-looking portal that reminds me of a small arched entryway to a Hobbit's house. I am in my own little cave.

My suitcase will serve as my closet, so it's not long before I've set up my cozy Hobbit-like home. I head back downstairs to see loads of beautiful faces from all over the world—women and nuns of all ages and ethnicities. Today is Saturday, the day of new arrivals, and many look just like me: wide-eyed and curious. The main gathering area is the dining hall, where there are rows of wooden tables, a tea and coffee station, and a welcoming fireplace. At the front of the room, there is a white board on which daily announcements are written in French, English, and Vietnamese.

The next moment, a gong rings—not the big one in the field, but a smaller one hanging just outside the entrance to the kitchen. It's a pleasant sound, and it signals the beginning of dinner. Meals are always eaten in silence for a period of twenty minutes. Following the others, I join the line of nuns and women standing before a long buffet table, spread with healthy-looking dishes of food. I put two big spoons of French green lentils onto a plate, add vermicelli noodles and steamed purple cabbage, and then pour dark brown miso gravy over the whole of it. I take a seat at one of the dining room tables, and then the anticipation comes. Something is definitely going to happen here. I'm not sure what, but it's going to start right now with these lentils. Over the next forty days, I will come to see the power and importance of prayer, mindfulness, and attention while eating.

A nun rings a gong, this one inside, and then she reads a prayer. We are now permitted to eat. The Sister that had greeted me earlier in the day, the one with the powerful wrestler scalp, is seated at the table across from me—her pulsating head muscles straight in my view.

Another Vietnamese Sister sits down right beside me, even though there are many empty places at the table. "The exact opposite of what would happen in any restaurant," I think. This cherubic-faced nun sits comfortably close. Looking me straight in the eyes, she smiles a wide, warm smile, presses her hands to her heart, and gently bows her head. My heart aches.

And the journey begins . . .

⇌ Day 1 ⇋

Body:
Taking Refuge Within
My Wise Self

*Men are born soft and supple; dead they are stiff and
hard . . .*
Thus whoever is stiff and inflexible is a disciple of death.
Whoever is soft and yielding is a disciple of life.
                                                    —TAO TE CHING

It's not a bad way to wake up; it's just so early. A Buddhist
nun is ringing a brass gong, and it's 5:00 a.m. My eyes
open, then immediately close. Can't get up. In fact, the
gong sounds rather pleasant. I could easily sleep through
its mesmerizing vibrations. To slip out from under my
warm blanket would mean to face head-on the chilly
air in my spare, monastic room. But meditation starts at
5:30 a.m, so I have to get moving—latecomers are not
allowed in the Buddha Hall. Eyes open again. This time
I brave the ice-cold air, wrap my ivory wool shawl over
my still-sore-from-traveling shoulders, and head down

the stairs of the residence onto the outdoor path leading to the Buddha Hall. The sun is still quiet.

I am now sitting on a square, navy blue cushion on the floor, in the first of eight vertical rows that stretch toward a magnificent, six-foot tall, white Buddha statue perched in a nook in the stone wall. There is a shrine of incense and flowers before it. Upon closer examination, I realize the Buddha is a salmon-pink color but the lights of the hall cause it to appear a brilliant white.

All the Sisters of New Hamlet and the visiting female pilgrims have gathered to chant, pray, breathe, and bow to the earth in reverence of the Buddha's great teachings. Good fortune has brought me here, and yet I can't help but wonder why the Sisters I see here chose this monastic life, essentially giving up, *for good*, romantic partners, having babies, café lattes with the *New York Times* on lazy Sunday mornings, and hot, lavender-scented baths. "And they get up at the crack of dawn every day," I think to myself during a moment of mind wandering. Instead, I should be thinking: *Breathing in, I am aware of my body. Breathing out, I release the tension in my body.* "And they will most probably rise early for the rest of their days." With this last thought, I gaze in admiration at the women sitting in meditation with me. And then I come back to the moment. *Breathing in, I am aware of my body. Breathing out, I release the tension in my body.* As I turn inward, my breath gradually becomes deep and slow. Attending to these languid whispers softens my body.

Later on, I will refer to nuns as women, only to be firmly reminded by a stern-looking Sister who reminds me of a tough-as-nails-nun from my Catholic school days that Sisters are not to be referred to as women—they are to be called Sisters or nuns.

The first of my forty days is a whirlwind of beautiful bald heads, earth-brown robes, resplendent chants, and majestic surroundings. My deep curiosity touches all of it. Plum Village is another universe.

After dinner and linden flower tea with my new British friend, who had journeyed here with me yesterday, the two of us take a walk outside to see the blackest of country skies filled with masses of luminous stars. The air smells like the earth, damp and rich and cool. I breathe in the density. Three more thick breaths, and my fatigue finally catches up to me. I say goodnight to my walking companion and head back to the residence.

At the end of this long first day, the only thing I want is a shower. I am now standing in a washroom so tiny that every time I turn I bump a body part into a wall. "But this shower will be glorious," I think. I can't wait for the steaming, hot water to pound on my tired back. Body undressed, tap turned on, expectant delight. But instead of a forceful stream of fiery water, out comes a tepid dribble. A frown crosses my brow. Into the shower stall I go anyway, under the illusion that *force of will* could fire up a water furnace. But—and I know you've already guessed it—the very minute I am covered in soap, the trickle that was there disappears. I am buck naked, wet, and shivering cold. Did I mention I have itchy soap suds all over my body? I glance down at my goose bumps. But I am at a monastery and maybe the air is just different here. In the few moments of standing and wondering what to do, I recall Thich Nhat Hanh's dictum, "Take refuge in your self." "Right, that's why I came here," I think, "to figure out how to take refuge in myself—no matter what is going on." I must not forget that the monk who uttered these true words is my guide on this journey. Simply recalling this relaxes me somewhat, and then my concentration sharpens. I think of my options. I can wrap my miniscule towel around my wet body and traipse down through the nun's quarters and into one of their showers. I quickly dismiss that idea. I can stand here and pray that the water will come back on. That seems dumb. Okay, how about this? I can follow the monk's suggestion and *come back to the island that is myself.*

So, here I am. It is ten o'clock. There's not a peep in the residence. Everyone is in bed, and I'm standing here tired, cold, wet, and naked, with soap suds covering my entire body, in a beige-walled shower stall with no running water. In a monastery. In France. There's nothing else to do but stand here and breathe. And then maybe, just maybe, some idea about what to do will miraculously appear. I stare at one beige wall of the rectangle shower box. An agile black spider crawls up one corner. She must be happy there's no water here. I focus on her shiny, ebony spider body. In the next moment I hear my breath. I bathe in the sound of my breathing. I listen to the damp air coming into my chest. I am soaked in the sensation of the following exhale. Inhale. Exhale. Stillness. Inhale. Exhale. Stillness. I know I am breathing. Within about sixty seconds, my gooseflesh softens. I am yielding. Somehow, I begin to accept my circumstances. Whether or not the water comes back on has nothing to do with me, so why fight it with stiffness and inflexibility? "And, furthermore, why do I battle against all the things in my life that I can't possibly control?" I am talking to the arachnid now. "I am able to rule my body, right? But I can't control my surroundings." I bring my face close to the now-motionless spider and examine her eight skinny, soap-free legs. "You know this, don't you? Why don't I always remember this?" I say it out loud, the ebony spider as my witness: "Take refuge in your self, Mary."

Eastern teachings state that your body is a microcosm of the universe. As you tune in to your body, you know your body. Then, because you have insight into that body (the microcosm), the workings of the world (the macrocosm) are revealed to you. Herein lies a great ability.

To master oneself is to master the world.

Think of all the things you do with your body. Earlier today I did a little weeding in the garden greenhouse in which the nuns grow organic fruits, vegetables, and herbs. This is one of the many working meditations that visitors are asked to partake in while staying at the monastery. At dinner, I relished the spinach and arugula leaves from that very garden. After a few too many butter croissants in Paris prior to my pilgrimage, even after just one day of eating nutrient-dense meals, I feel lightness in my body and renewed clarity in my mind.

The food we put into our bodies influences our mind and impacts our health. That is why, here at Plum Village, careful attention is paid to the quality of all meals. Too much sugar, like sickly sweet donuts, and we see everything through a curtain of fog; too much spice (watch the chilies!), and we can't concentrate during meditation; overeating makes us sleepy. Everything we ingest affects us in some way. There is something else—the wrong type of food can produce deep tension inside our bodies. It is difficult to come back to the island that is yourself if that island is full of pain. Who wants to visit an abode of suffering?

Relishing these wholesome culinary delights today, I wonder why I don't have the discipline to consistently eat well at home. Salt and vinegar potato chips make my muscles hurt—like they are crying out for real nutrition. In just twenty-four hours, being at the monastery has awakened me to my own misery. I realize now that I slip in and out of treating my body with the respect it deserves.

Thich Nhat Hanh says that the physical tension existing in our bodies is "a kind of suffering." Pain will eventually cause illness unless we have an effective technique to release that pressure on a regular basis. "We should always try to be compassionate toward ourselves, then we will understand how to reduce the pain we carry within." Thây speaks of *taking refuge within our self*, of *going home to ourselves* through the act of mindful breathing. This conscious breath technique, which the Buddha counseled as a prescription to rid ourselves of our suffering, unifies our mind and body so that we become established in the here and now. I take the first of many silent vows: "I'm determined to remember to breathe mindfully."

So who is the Buddha? Who is this *being* who has influenced countless people, not to mention Thich Nhat Hanh?

The enlightened Being we now call the Buddha was once a man named Siddhartha Gautama who lived in India over 2,500 years ago. This young man was a seeker. He wanted to understand the nature of existence and human life. After six years of intense practice with several renowned spiritual teachers, Siddhartha sat under a Boddhi tree and vowed not to stand up until he was enlightened. He sat all night; then as the morning star arose, he had a breakthrough that filled him with understanding and love. He became enlightened. After enjoying his realization for forty-nine days, the Buddha walked to Deer Park in Sarnath and joined five of his fellow ascetics. As Thich Nhat Hanh recounts in *The Heart of the Buddha's Teachings*, the Buddha then proclaimed some version of the following teaching: "I have seen deeply that nothing can be by itself alone, that everything has to *inter-be* with everything else. I have also seen that all beings are endowed with the nature of awakening."

The Buddha then taught The Four Noble Truths:

1. There is the existence of suffering.
2. There is the making of suffering.
3. There is a way out of that suffering.
4. There is a specific path to restore well-being called The Noble Eightfold Path.

> "Wherever the Noble Eightfold Path is practiced, joy, peace and insight are there."[1]

---

[1] *Mahaparinibbana Sutta, Digha Nikaya*, 16.

Thich Nhat Hanh emphasizes that this Noble Path of Eight Limbs——. Right View, Right Thinking, Right Speech, Right Action, Right Livelihood, Right Diligence, Right Mindfulness, and Right Concentration—are of the nature of inter-being. The Zen master notes that "each limb contains all the other seven."

Since I am here to apply the Buddha's teachings, and now that I am gratefully lying in my warm bed, I ponder that frustrating, albeit minor, upset of my inaugural monastic shower. I was distressingly tired, wet, and cold. This was evidence of The First Noble Truth—I was suffering. That's pretty straightforward. My aversion to the lack of water was The Second Noble Truth—that is, there was a reason I was suffering and that reason was I hated being freezing cold and wet! But there are always choices. Faced with no water in the shower, I could either have fought that reality or accepted my circumstances. The fact that I understood through mindfulness that it was possible to reduce my discomfort proves The Third Noble Truth—there was a way out of suffering. Then, choosing to concentrate on my moving breath brought some relief from my frustration, as well as some insight. I knew my discomfort was impermanent. Nothing lasts—no pain, no pleasure. My concentrated breathing brought me back to the island that is myself, where many resources and insights exist. In this case, the recognition of the simple truth that no water in a shower is a very minor upset. There is a freedom in recognizing when you have absolutely no control in a situation. Acceptance is entirely liberating, as is resolve. My frustration was instantly cut in half. I touched The Fourth Noble Truth, the path that restored my well-being.

Today I glimpsed the immense possibilities of mindfulness. "I can see that coming back to the island that is myself, this taking refuge within, is empowering and liberating," I muse. But I wonder if I will be able to go there when a more difficult situation arises. That is the real question.

The Buddha did not say that everything *is* suffering as many interpret his teachings to mean. Thich Nhat Hanh said that the main aim of the Buddha was to *transform* suffering. "You must find the ill-being within yourself and then transform it."

The water in my shower eventually came back on, the black spider crawled away, and I happily rinsed off the soap suds. When we relax, things have a way of turning out.

☞ Day 2 ☜

Beginner's Mind: Conquering My Boredom

The cure for boredom is curiosity. There is no cure for curiosity.

—DOROTHY PARKER

I am at the dining room table having dinner. Across from me sits a stunningly beautiful young Vietnamese nun. Her full lips and prominent cheekbones grace a perfectly golden visage. Even with her bald head and dull, brown robes, she is breathtaking. For a moment, I think about shaving my head. I wonder if the nun's beauty mesmerizes the monks. I can't take my eyes off of her. A thought crosses my mind. Perhaps monks and nuns have achieved the ultimate escape—that is, from romantic relationships.

I once left a deeply loving relationship with a close to perfect man. At the time, I thought I had moved on to seek higher ideals, but I see now it was simply out of boredom. I realize this much more clearly here, far away from home, in a Buddhist monastery, sitting across from the beautiful young nun. "What was the real cause of my lethargy?" I silently wonder. What was this ennui that I had felt with Mr. Wonderful? Thich Nhat Hanh might say that I had lost my mind—my "beginner's mind," that is. He might just say that I had forgotten what I so enjoyed about this man who had loved me perhaps more fully than any other had. Thây teaches that forgetfulness is the opposite of mindfulness and that we are made of these two conflicts. And when our forgetfulness dominates the picture, we absolutely do not have a beginner's mind.

Years ago, at a meditation retreat, I learned how to be mindful during my daily activities. As I brushed my teeth, for example, I concentrated just on that task. While washing my hands, walking, or eating lunch, I attempted to quiet my chattering mind and immerse myself fully in one action at one time. As I became mindful, I realized that I hadn't always completely concentrated on these everyday activities. Because such actions were so very regular, I had done them with a degree of mindlessness. But whenever I paid close attention to what I was doing, no matter what the activity, something changed within. I felt less *outside of myself*. I identified more with my inner energy. In yogic terms, this energy is often called *life force*, *chi*, or *prana*. In simple terms, mindfulness connected me to my true self. Whenever I was able to be mindful, every moment felt new—because it was—and there was nothing for my habitual mind to grasp on to. I wasn't mindlessly eating a cheese sandwich in the present while, say, worrying about my landlord not fixing the leaky roof at my yoga studio, for example. Being engaged in one action at one time kept me from fantasizing about some far away golden future. These present-moment awakenings were fleeting, but the more I concentrated, the more the flashes came. And when they arrived, it felt very good—like I was living life, not ruminating, thinking, or fantasizing about life. Time goes by in a flash, yet strangely we act as if we will live forever. Waking up to the moment shines a powerful spotlight on this reality. Here at the monastery, I am reminded yet again of the life-enriching power of sharp concentration.

So here I am, with the innocent beauty, in a far-away monastery, thinking about what it means to truly know exactly what I am doing in every moment. It's not easy. But I do know that if I can be as mindful as possible, I will be released from my nagging, habitual, and agonizingly repetitive thoughts on everything from craving some impossibly perfect man to ruminating on the vicissitudes of romantic relationships. With those thoughts cleared away, I can be in my life, even through the most mundane of tasks. I can experience life, not fruitlessly regret things of the past, and not worry about what is yet to come. Somehow, this is just how it works.

Dinner has finished and the beautiful nun has left the table. She has joined some of her Sisters to clean the dining hall. I sit here with my cup of yellow tea and watch them with their bright sponges and old-fashioned straw brooms. In the coming days, I will have this working meditation. But not tonight. As I watch them, all of these quiet beings, without exception, seem carefully focused on their task in a way that looks different from how I usually clean. Nothing else is on their minds—I can see that on their faces. There are no frowns—no signals of brooding thoughts. These sharp-minded beings are purely and simply sweeping the floor.

I remember the mystic Sadhguru saying something like, our problem is that we are using every activity to *enhance* who we are rather than *dissolve* who we are. We do things for ourselves in the best of ways, but not for others. We sweep our own floor better than we sweep our friend's floor. These nuns clearly do not have this troublesome quality.

I take another sip of chamomile tea and decide that the forgetful mind often dominates the beginner's mind because we let the commonplace become routine. We lack an appreciation of the significance of continued mindfulness—especially during so-called mundane activities, like scrubbing a dining hall floor. Bearing witness to the cleanup crew of nuns, I am reminded that it does not have to be that way. It is true that this conflict of forgetfulness and mindfulness is inherent in the human experience, but Thich Nhat Hanh teaches that as you foster mindfulness, you leap over your conflicted mind.

Back home at my yoga studio, while teaching, I have often seen some of my students approaching familiar poses as if they were casually doing a sit-up. They may have practiced a certain posture hundreds of times, and thus have become too familiar with it. That pose then lacks power. The students are shaping their bodies, but they are not really *in* the pose. If approached with careless familiarity, even a practice meant to improve mindfulness can feed the beast of forgetfulness.

In an article for the Buddhist journal *the Shambhala Sun*, Thây elaborates on beginner's mind using the common activity of tea drinking:

> There have been many times you have been drinking tea and didn't know it, because you were absorbed in worries . . . . If you don't know how to drink your tea in mindfulness and concentration, you are not really drinking tea. You are drinking your sorrow, your fear, your anger—and happiness is not possible.

How many times have we drunk our sorrow? We drink our tea but worry about something else. In this illuminating passage, we see how joy can come by simply being mindful during an everyday act. That attentiveness ignites happiness in that moment, but it also creates mindfulness in all areas of our lives because when we *really* drink our tea, we are practicing how to be aware of *all* that we do. Thây teaches that in order for great insight to be possible, this type of concentration must be nurtured all the time. If we train ourselves to live in such a way, happiness and insight will continue to grow. Then our sorrows and fears weaken.

I look into the cup of golden tea in my hands. "I must continually call to mind the importance of sharp attention," I think. It is clear but so very difficult.

I once attended a workshop on conscious communication taught by a man who had been married for forty years. After the course, a student approached this teacher with a question: "Sir, how is it that you don't get bored being with the same woman for so many years?" The teacher replied: "I don't know what you mean; please explain." The student tried again: "Well, don't you crave variety sometimes?" The teacher again questioned: "I still don't understand you. I'm sorry, what is it that you are asking?" The student: "Sir, if I may say so, aren't there times when you just want to be with another woman?" The teacher queried: "What do you mean exactly, *be* with another woman?" The now nervous student asked: "Yes sir, I mean don't you ever want to, you know, *sleep* with another woman?" And the teacher replied: "Why would I want to sleep with another woman? My wife has about three hundred personalities and I think I've discovered maybe a hundred of them. Every day I wake up excited about seeing another aspect of her!"

Even though Thich Nhat Hanh has been a monk since the age of sixteen, his insight into romantic relationships is incredible. In an article for *the Shambhala Sun*, he counseled:

> Look into the eyes of your beloved and ask,
> 'Who are you, my darling?' Ask with your
> whole being. If you do not give right attention

17

to the one you love, it is a kind of killing. If you are lost in your thoughts, assuming you know everything about her, she will slowly die. But with mindfulness, you will be able to discover many new and wonderful things— her joys, her hidden talents, her deepest aspirations. If you do not practice appropriate attention, how can you say you love her?

The floor of the dining hall is now gleaming, and the joyous monastic cleanup crew have placed the mops and sponges in the closet. I am the sole person in the hall. The blue embers in the fireplace hypnotize as I continue to ponder this most challenging of Buddhist states of being—beginner's mind. The magic of children is in their ability to deeply immerse themselves in everything; life is new to these young beings. As adults, we generally only have this kind of attention while learning a skill, launching into a novel venture, or beginning a romantic relationship. As things and people become familiar, we often lose interest. I wonder about this waning enthusiasm, and have a moment of sadness—just one of many I will experience here.

I realize that I must treat all living beings like they are as precious and special and mysterious as my very first true love. I must have a deep curiosity about all life here on earth. I think now about how to better hone that curiosity.

Albert Einstein said: "The important thing is not to stop questioning. Curiosity has its own reason for existing. One cannot help but be in awe when one contemplates the mysteries of eternity, of life, of the marvelous structure of reality. It is enough if one tries merely to comprehend a little of this mystery every day. Never lose a holy curiosity."

If I am fully present as I walk on the earth, how can I cause destruction to it? If I am mindful during all of my activities, how can I *not* create excellence? If I know my lover is a supremely complex being, how can I not want to know everything about him—while recognizing the impossibility of that as stimulating? If I am aware that I will die someday, how can I waste a single moment? I cannot. Just like the man who was married for forty years, joyfully discovering his wife's myriad personalities, I will discover beauty and complexity as I become fully cognizant of my relationship with all living beings and the mysteries yet to be discovered.

The fire is breathing its last breath and my teacup is empty. I get up from the fireside bench to realize that in the space of two hours, a beautiful nun and a bunch of happy Buddhist Sisters cleaning a dining hall floor with Zen fervor have shown me the wisdom in approaching everything in life with fresh, child-like eyes. At the very least, fostering a curious beginner's mind could very well keep long-term romantic relationships alive with the joy of constant discovery. That would be a wonderful thing.

↜ Day 3 ↝

Ethical Mind (*Sila*):
The Cat Killer

*Let me give you the definition of ethics: It is good to main-
tain life and further life. It is bad to damage and destroy
life. And this ethic, profound and universal, has the significance of a religion. It is a religion.*

—ALBERT SCHWEITZER

"Killing the cats was fucking killing me."
I am sitting in the late afternoon sunlight, in the
monk's gardens, looking into a set of twinkling blue eyes
belonging to a man who's telling me that six years ago, self-
destruction was near. You wouldn't think it, looking at my
fellow pilgrim now—a sixty-ish, easygoing, friendly man
from Newfoundland. Anyone who wears a multi-colored,
embroidered, Mexican poncho must be relaxed, right?
But Charlie admits that he wasn't always carefree. "I was
raised to be a trained killer," he says. Growing up, Charlie was encouraged to kill animals for sport. This killing
continued with his chosen profession, neuropsychology.

Charlie's work involved stimulating different parts of cats' brains to observe how they reacted to fear. This research was carried out on felines in order to shed light on the fear response in the human brain. "Torturing cats was pretty bad. But that wasn't the worst of it." Charlie goes on to say that each experiment involved killing the cat afterward to remove and dissect the brain.

It was a book by Thich Nhat Hanh that changed Charlie's life. Charlie has now been a practitioner of Zen mindfulness and meditation for eight years. This former slayer of cats spoke to me about Thây's Five Mindfulness Trainings. These trainings transformed Charlie's life. Particularly significant for him was the First Mindfulness Training—Reverence for Life, a tenet illuminating the problems inherent in destroying life. Two days from now, I will read this teaching myself.

Earlier today, before meeting Charlie with the twinkling blue eyes, I had been sitting amongst a group of pilgrims in the front room of New Hamlet. I listened to a young woman who was a chef-in-training back in Canada as she revealed a history of crustacean-killing through staccato sobs. "My lobster just went limp, almost like it knew the end was coming, and there was nothing it could do about it. The other chef's lobster reacted in the opposite way. It fought to the bitter end. Did you know that lobsters wail as they are being boiled alive?"

<hr>

Shortly after I returned home from France, while grocery shopping one evening, I walked by a tank holding live lobsters. Gazing at these unlucky crustaceans, I immediately recalled my conversation with the young "chef in training" from Plum Village. There I was, jars of peanut butter to my left, live lobsters to my right, frozen in a grocery mart amongst my fellow shoppers who were, of course, ignoring the imprisoned invertebrates. I stood there, looking at those pale grey and mottled-brown bottom feeders piled on top of each other and rendered helpless by blue rubber bands constraining leaden pincers.

I've always thought it somewhat torturous to strap bands around the claws of live shellfish and pile them, bound and aimless, in tanks the size of small aquariums. I know that they have miniscule brains, but that reality has not been enough to stop me from occasionally eating their butter-dipped flesh. And although lobsters do not have vocal chords—they cannot scream—the sound they make while they are being boiled alive is simply steam being released from between their body and its shell— dropping them into piping hot water seems like persecution. I read recently that zoologists have confirmed that lobsters have a very sensitive tactile sense and boiling takes between thirty-five to forty-five seconds to kill them. Lobsters feel pain. We boil them alive. I think I'll pass on future surf and turf meals.

That same night, after returning home from the lobster jail, I decided to watch a documentary called *Sharkwater*. In the film, it was revealed that in some regions, sharks are being caught solely for their fins to make soup. Shark fin soup is a Chinese delicacy served at weddings and other special occasions. This luxury item is considered a symbol of wealth and prestige in Chinese culture. A bowl of shark fin soup can cost up to $90. The increasingly high demand for this strange delicacy has caused a sharp increase in the practice known as shark finning. The film showed local fishermen off the coast of Costa Rica, slicing the fins from sharks and throwing their useless bodies back into the ocean. Unable to swim, the massacred creatures sink and ultimately suffocate to death. The image of a shark brutally sliced and sinking to a silent death wrenched me in my gut. No matter what misperception we have of sharks, this informative documentary revealed the truth about this necessary predator in our oceans. Sharks help maintain the delicate balance between all the marine life in the seas. When the numbers of these massive fish reduce dramatically, every-thing else is impacted. Killing sharks ultimately endangers our lives.

That night, well after my journey, I thought again about the nature of an ethical, reverent, insightful mind. This is an awakened mind—the mind that embodies the understanding that all life is interconnected and comes from one source, and that other creatures sustain human lives. With this mind, it is difficult to kill. If we are mind-ful, we are naturally moral. If we feel our connection with others, do we then need to be told not to cause harm?

Thich Nhat Hanh emphasizes the great importance of being mindful: "Right Mindfulness is at the heart of the Buddha's teachings." And while proper mindful-ness simply means "remembering" or being truly aware of what is there in the moment, to gain Right Mindful-ness, the Buddha offered four objects for our practice: the body, feelings, mind, and objects of the mind, as contained in the Satipatthana Sutta. In *The Heart of the Buddha's Teachings*, Thich Nhat Hanh notes of these four practices: "Without them, our house is abandoned; no one is sweeping, dusting or tidying up. Our body becomes unkempt, our feelings full of suffering, and our mind a heap of afflictions."

What stood out for me while listening to Thây talk about the Buddha's teachings on mindfulness was the Zen master's emphasis on Right Mindfulness being equal to ethical living, or its Buddhist term, *Sila*. Thây has helped me to see mindfulness and ethics as basically interchangeable. That is, if we are truly aware, we will be moral. If we are cognizant of our actions, it is only natu-ral to be ethical. The problem is that we often obscure our view by acting in a bit of a fog. Thây emphasizes the interconnected nature of mindfulness and the Buddha's moral precepts: "The heart of Buddhist meditation *is* the practice of mindfulness, and mindfulness *is* the practice of the precepts. You cannot meditate without practicing the precepts." And there it is—practice makes perfect. Countless Catholic school days of being instructed, "Thou shalt not kill" did not cause me to embody that tenet, whereas the activity of meditation brought me to a state of knowing that I should not kill living beings. The lobsters will be happy.

Back at the monastery, Charlie the cat killer, his poncho, and I are happily nibbling leftover almond cookies from lunch in the sunlit garden. Charlie tells me that he quit his work soon after discovering the teachings of Thich Nhat Hanh. He felt terrible about being a cat killer. Charlie tells me that he was desperately unhappy during this time; he was falling into deep depressive states. And it wasn't only the executions of cats that unmoored the Newfoundlander. Charlie's personal relationships were rocky and he had two collapsed marriages behind him. He also admitted that at the height of his restlessness, he was in intimate relationships with three women at the same time. There was even one occasion when two of the women turned up at the same party, while the third one simultaneously called his mobile phone. Talk about stressful. Charlie revealed that his complicated personal life had been extremely distressing, and that soon his whole life would spiral down. He had accumulated a vast amount of debt and was facing bankruptcy. At the peak of his unrest, Charlie said that he knew something had to change or he feared he would literally self-destruct.

Charlie now looks at me with open blue eyes and says that on the brink of total collapse, he had a glimmer of insight. He decided to sell a property he owned in Newfoundland that had gone up in value a great deal since his original purchase. The profit from the sale covered all his debt, and he then wisely controlled his spending.

Charlie now enjoys a far less complicated life with no drinking, no meat eating, and only one girlfriend with whom he has had a stable, loving relationship for four years. Together, they regularly host writing workshops and meditation gatherings at their home. Charlie, good Newfoundlander that he is, also has a fine way with a song, reminding me of my beloved sister-in-law, Janice.

I say good-bye to Charlie and walk back toward the residence, thinking about the opportunity that everyone has to go home to an enduring, clear-minded self no matter where we are, because our mind is with us always. Fostering clarity and being mindful, we are moral. Then we don't have to be taught what is right and wrong. Like the reformed cat killer, through the practice of mindfulness, morality comes naturally.

☙ Day 4 ☙

Focused Mind (*Samadhi*): The Day the Monk Lit Up My Spine

All the resources we need are in the mind.

—THEODORE ROOSEVELT

Thây is holding a delicate yellow rose in his fingers: "If you are mindful of the rose, then you also have some concentration on the rose. When you are mindful of the rose and concentrated on the rose, then you know the rose—you have some insight into that rose." In one brief phrase, Thich Nhat Hanh has encapsulated the complex Buddhist teachings known as *Sila*, *Samadhi*, and *Prajna*, which translate to "mindfulness," "concentration," and "insight."

Thich Nhat Hanh teaches that it is crucial to understand the interconnection and interdependence between these three teachings. "The energy of concentration is contained in mindfulness, just as the energy of insight is contained in concentration." He wrote this on the blackboard: mindfulness ⇔ concentration ⇔ insight.

Following this pathway leads to a breakthrough into the nature of reality—in this case, the truth of the rose.

❦

Up until now, Thich Nhat Hanh has been a revered presence in the distance. I caught a glimpse of him when he welcomed all of the pilgrims to his monastery during the opening ceremonies of the retreat, but today I will see the Zen master close up. I am sitting on the floor at the front of the Buddha Hall in Upper Hamlet with the kind of anticipation felt before a famous rock star walks onto a stage. But here, in this substitute stadium, I will be much closer to the Buddhist heavyweight than I was to, say, Chris Martin of Coldplay earlier this year. I am sitting on a navy blue cushion in the second row of the concert hall of the Buddha. Behind me are rows upon rows of monks and nuns, men and women, all sitting on their own blue cushions. To my right is the door through which Thich Nhat Hanh will enter.

The room goes quiet. In the next moment, like magic, a deceptively diminutive figure in a long brown robe melts into the room without a sound. The intuitive being slips out of his shoes while removing a brown toque and handing it to an attending monk. The eighty-four-year-old Zen master has large, wise-looking ears that appear like two magnificent sculptures framing the insightful doorway that is the monk's face. Thich Nhat Hanh looks as if he has seen things—things that not many of us have seen. Thây also appears perhaps fifteen years younger than his age. Can I call an eighty-four-year-old Vietnamese monk cute? The transcendent face before me has that childlike quality. Is this the look of enlightenment? Thây doesn't expressly survey the group of many hundreds of people here, but that will change when he begins to speak. As Thây utters his first phrase, in an instant, I will feel as if he is talking directly to me.

Thich Nhat Hanh glides over to the podium. My eyes follow every subtle movement of the floating figure.

The monk hasn't said a thing, yet I am riveted. He gently plucks a yellow rose from a vase, turns, and says: "A rose is not a rose; that is why it is a real rose."

And then it happens. I've felt it at other times in my life, but it always delights me. I become suffused with a warm, buzzing sensation at the level of my spine, between my shoulder blades. A little smile starts on my lips. Here I am in a room full of hundreds of strangers, with a secret—a vibrating spine. I blissfully think, "Everything makes sense." In this moment, I have all I would ever need to feel secure. The Buddhist rock star has sung.

I'm sure there are other people here with their own hidden delights. But, I am so focused on the gliding monk—the one who has lit up my spine—that I mostly feel surprisingly light. I am in my own warm bubble. My entire body softens, and I think: "Thank God for Thich Nhat Hanh."

Later on, I reflect on my first experience in the presence of Thich Nhat Hanh. Perhaps because it is almost Christmas, an image of the Grinch from my favorite Christmas cartoon, *How the Grinch Stole Christmas!*, comes to mind. In the story, there is a moment when the Grinch watches the residents of Whoville celebrating the coming of Christmas even though all their presents are gone—stolen by the Grinch himself. On a snow-covered mountaintop, this grumpy creature has an epiphany. Gazing down at the peaceful faces in the village, he realizes that Christmas has nothing to do with presents. This festival is about celebrating love, community, union, and gratitude for life itself. In that miraculous moment, the Grinch's "Christ-consciousness" awakens, represented by his heart expanding in his chest. His face wondrously lights up, and at once he understands the truth: that love and compassion cause happiness.

I gaze at the equation on the board in front of me, and furiously write it down: mindfulness ⇔ concentration ⇔ insight.

Here it is. These three dense words represent the ideal way of being. The arrows between them reveal their interdependence and connection: if I am mindful, if I am aware of what is there, I will enhance my concentration, which will bring insight into the object of my focus. Thây has placed the rose back in the vase. I again look at the flower. It appears different from non-flower things. But then I look at the flower very deeply, and I can see that there are "non-flower" components to the yellow rose. That wisdom is like breaking through into the nature of reality. The truth is that everything is simply made up of things that it is not—a yellow rose flower is simply a bunch of non-yellow-rose-flower things coming together to create a beautiful, fragrant plant with lovely petals. The rose is just a combination of sunshine, clouds, time, earth, minerals, air, gardeners, and so on. Without all of these "non-flower" elements, the flower cannot exist. When we remove our concept of a rose, we see the real rose. With this understanding of what Buddhists call "non-self," it is possible to become liberated from despair and confusion.

Thây explains that because of their interconnectedness, the three disciplines of mindfulness, concentration, and insight support each other—they make each other more solid. So, when one of them is improved, the other two automatically strengthen.

These important teachings are three components of the Noble Eightfold Path: eight specific steps the Buddha identified as leading to well being. I was introduced to these on the first day of my pilgrimage. Thây now emphasizes that when one of these components, the pivotal element of mindfulness, is the right *kind* of mindfulness, then the other seven elements of the Noble Eightfold

Path are also present, along with an understanding of the Four Noble Truths. Right Mindfulness—Sila is the base of it all. This state of mind is the energy that brings us back to the present moment where everything happens.

❧ ☙

I think of how often I've let my concentration slip, or the times when I've done something without thinking of the potential consequences of that action, or the other times when I've just done something dumb. Here, in the presence of Thây, I close my eyes and concentrate deeply on his words. "It is easy to do this here," I decide. If I can remember this feeling and practice this kind of focus in all that I think, say, and do, wherever I may be—well, that would be something. If I could do that, then I would always know that my actions have specific repercussions. I would have an idea whether or not a particular act is a moral one—a mindful one. Of course the choice is always there. But the message is simple: if I lack real awareness in my common, everyday activities, then I act without considering my impact on other people and all living beings in the world. If I don't understand what I am doing, how can I have a moral dilemma about my actions; how can I care?

Thây has finished his talk and has melted out of the room. I want to be by myself now, and so I walk silently on the pristine grounds of Upper Hamlet, with the yellow flowers and purple plums the monks are so fortunate to live amongst. During my stroll, I think of all the people in the world who are successful in what they do. "Accomplished people are able to deeply focus their minds, and that makes them excel at their craft. A concentrated mind is just as crucial as a beginner's mind to actualize quality." I expand this thought in my mind. "And not only that, but this kind of one-pointed mind is highly cognizant of its actions and the repercussions of those actions."

My science-loving mind now turns to the work of ant biologist Deborah Gordon. I think of her strong mind as a Samadhi kind of mind. Deborah Gordon spent twenty-five years observing and charting ant colonies in the Arizona desert. What she discovered was contrary to the existing popular notion that ant colonies evolved into organized systems. Instead Deborah saw a system driven by accident, adaptation, and chaos. This is important because the aggregate system of the ant colony can shed light on the evolution of other aggregate systems, including the human brain (which evolved from a simple neuron to a complex cortex). Simply put, we can learn about our own human complexity by observing an ant. Gordon's astounding ability to concentrate is the kind of mind that is an invaluable resource for the world.

Ants are incredible. After I returned home from my pilgrimage, I came across the astonishing fact that the ten thousand trillion ants in the world, as calculated in 2007 by biologist E.O. Wilson, together weigh roughly as much as the 6.5 billion human beings. I wonder if the ants are multiplying as fast as the seven billion human bodies rolling around on the planet in 2011.

Squishing a purple plum under my foot as I walk on this fertile ground, I think of exceptionally skilled musicians as having this Samadhi kind of mind as well. I once had a brilliant violin player taking yoga and meditation classes from me. Luke's interest in meditation sprang from a spontaneous awakening he had experienced while sitting on a big rock by a lake. Luke told me that as he focused his mind on the body of water in front of him, and the vast blue sky, he forgot himself. For a moment, time stood still. He felt that he *was* the water. He *became* the open, endless sky. Luke said that this feeling was fleeting, yet glorious. And he knew that it had had something to do with concentrating his mind one-pointedly on the nature surrounding him in those moments. Luke's epiphany had caused him to be intensely curious about the nature of his mind.

Thich Nhat Hanh emphasizes the vital importance of applying the Buddha's teachings to modern life. So, as I continue to walk, I take a moment to apply the Buddha's teachings to the ant biologist. When Deborah Gordon is mindful of the ant, she will also have some concentration on the ant. Because she is mindful of the ant and concentrates on the ant, she knows the ant. She gains insight into that ant. With that wisdom, Gordon has a better idea of the ant's purpose—she has gained a breakthrough into the nature of reality. I imagine that exploring ants was liberating for Deborah Gordon. Her study also gave her valuable insight into humanity. Then it became natural for her to respect little bugs. It is the same for Luke, the musician. As he concentrated on expertly plucking the strings of the violin, he became more aware, more mindful of his craft. Because he was mindful, because he concentrated, insight came. He gained more knowledge about both the art of creating music and the violin itself. Every virtuoso violinist will tell you about the importance of the quality of the wood used to create a violin and the violin-making skill of the luthier—these are the "non-violin" elements of the violin. Again, just as a rose is simply made up of non-rose elements, a violin is also a bunch of things that it is not. A violin is made from non-violin things coming together to act as a violin. The gift of insight comes to me as more purple plums squash under my feet. Next comes the breakthrough in my understanding that absolutely everything is simply a combination of things that it is not—the Buddha's teaching on non-self. It rings very true for me in this moment.

As I finish my walk, I see the application of the Buddha's teachings in all of these people. Whether one is a biologist like Deborah Gordon or a musician like my yoga student Luke or a ballet dancer, carpenter, writer, architect, florist, poker player, or beekeeper is not the important thing. What matters is depth of concentration.

Just like Einstein proclaimed: "the journey of exploration and discovery is reason enough to pursue answers."

Today is the first of many days of Grinch-like heart-buzzing epiphanies for me. Hopefully, I am less Grinch-like than the pre-epiphany Grinch. And perhaps I am starting with a tad more awareness than the grumpy green creature. Nonetheless, I change in the presence of Thich Nhat Hanh. Listening to this gentle monk's words of wisdom, spoken from a place of deep concern for all beings, awakens love and insight within me on this precious day—my humming heart tells me so.

My House is getting organized.

I will never forget the gentle monk, holding the yellow rose.

☞ Day 5 ☜

Insightful Mind (*Prajna*):
The Lesson in a Bad Fish

Wisdom is ofttimes nearer when we stoop than when we soar.

—WILLIAM WORDSWORTH

W hen I was twenty years old, I went on holiday with a boyfriend to the Brazilian coastal city of Recife. One evening, while walking hand in hand on the beach in front of our hotel, three street children surrounded us and the oldest of them pointed a gun at our chests.

～☜ ☞～

It is late afternoon, and I am lying on my bed reading *The Heart of the Buddha's Teachings*. Thich Nhat Hanh is describing an incident during the Vietnam War when an American soldier spat on a novice monk, upsetting him deeply. This monk, the first ever to be ordained by Thây, had been so wounded that the fatherly monk had to gently hold the youth in his arms for a full thirty minutes to transform that feeling of deep hurt. Thich Nhat Hanh then explained to the novice that he must not hate the American soldier. He said, "My child, you were not born to hold a gun. You were born to be a monk, and your power is the power of understanding and love. The American soldier considered you to be his enemy. That was a wrong perception of his."

As I read this passage now, I think of what it must be like to be trained to kill. The U.S. Army conditioned that soldier to believe it was right to kill the Vietnamese. And that became the American soldier's view.

It was during the Vietnam War that Thich Nhat Hanh wrote the Five Mindfulness Trainings—tenets for ethical living. In 2009, Thây revised the trainings. The following is the new version of the First Training—Reverence for Life:

> I am determined not to kill, not to let others kill, and not to condone any act of killing in the world, in my thinking, or in my way of life. Seeing that harmful actions arise from anger, fear, greed, and intolerance, which in turn come from dualistic and discriminative thinking, I will cultivate openness, non-discrimination, and non-attachment to views in order to transform violence, fanaticism, and dogmatism in myself and in the world.

This is also the tenet that had changed a miserable, cat-killing philanderer into a happy, poncho-wearing meditator.

It is a direct message: wrong thinking is the foundation of killing. I have never thought about it that deeply before. If someone had asked me why people kill other people, I would have probably said that there were many reasons for this kind of violence. But, like many great masters, Thây is able to distill complex issues down to their purest core. "In war, there is a closed or wrong view that people are separate from each other. The proponents of war do not see that we are all intricately connected. This ignorance intensifies fear and anger. And then a dangerous attachment to notions develops. That attachment triggers violence." I close the book, and my eyes.

"Why would a child point a gun at me? Children should be playing." This was my thought after the incident in Brazil, back in the safe confines of my hotel. But later, of course, I realized that these poverty-stricken children were able to get their hands on and readily use these weapons because they were desperate to survive.

As I look back now, I can see the web that had led the Brazilian street children toward violence. Thây has enabled me to look more carefully at the flawed perspective that we are all subject to have. Of course young children are not personally responsible for developing mistaken beliefs, but they can grow up to develop erroneous views in a place like a favela in Brazil. Some young people don't have the luxury of simply playing. "An act of violence is not the fault of the child, and it is easy to forgive a child—they can't possibly know what they are doing," I think. "But Thây can forgive a soldier, a free-thinking adult who decides to humiliate a gentle monk." Thây immediately understood that the American soldier was not to blame for that cruel act of spitting on a peaceful Buddhist monk. The brilliance of Thich Nhat Hanh is that everything is so crystal clear to him. No one *person* is to blame for anything. What a liberating vision.

After Thây's Dharma talk earlier this morning, a senior monk stood up and said that there would be a question and answer period with Thây, an extremely rare event. A handsome young Australian man immediately raised his hand. He had a pressing question for

Thây, it seemed. A few days from today, I will hear this same man admit to treating women terribly. He will say this to a large group of us here, during an examination of the Third Mindfulness Training—which is about sexual responsibility. Upon hearing of his irreverent escapades, I will become thankful for the deeply respectful boyfriends of my past.

The Australian stood up and simply asked whether or not he should become a monk. His question took me by surprise. With his chiseled jaw, the conflicted man announced that he had aspirations to become monastic, but had recently been feeling a strong resistance and desire to go home. He then looked directly at Thây and asked, "Should I stay or should I go?"

Now, you might guess that a monk, himself finding the monastic path useful, would encourage others in the same direction, but Thich Nhat Hanh replied, "To stay or go makes no difference." I loved that he said that. "This is not the question. The question is: Can you look deep inside yourself, touch your feelings, recognize them, and then ultimately understand that your perception is partial? You then must observe other parts of your view. You must not be caught in your one view or any other outlook. You must allow your vision to be open; then you will eventually come to a good decision."

I wasn't expecting this intricate or wise an answer, but Thich Nhat Hanh's ability to catapult us to the summit of understanding is becoming clear to me now.

Thây went on to use the example of a fish swimming in water to expand on this teaching:

> The direction from which you look at something is your view. That is why it is called a point of view. If you were to look at a fish from the front, you would see the fish head, and that would be your *point of view*

of the fish. Another person may look at the fish from the tail and thus see it from that angle. Looking at the side of the fish creates another image. There are several views of the fish. But ultimately, with your one set of eyes, you are unable to see the whole fish at one time. Thus, in a sense, you are caught in your particular notion of the fish.

As Thây spoke, I closed my eyes and understood that I *only* look from my perspective. Thây continued, "If you believe in *only* your one view, then you think that other views are wrong."

I imagined a silvery fish. If I were to have a vice grip on the left fin of this imaginary fish, for example, then my mind would essentially be locked, and I would have no clue as to how the rest of the fish appeared. So, what to do? Thây advised us: "If you listen to other views, you will learn from these views." I thought of the famous saying, "Put yourself in someone else's shoes." I looked to my far right toward a monk at the other end of the hall. If this fictional "fish" were at the front of the room, my monastic friend would have seen a vastly different fish-shape than me, from my place on the left side of the room. Thây continued to illuminate us: "Learning from other views, you transcend your one view. Releasing your own view will give you deep insight. You will see the *totality of all views*." But in order to let this happen, he finally said, "You must be able to *truly* let go of your particular vision."

You must be humble or you will never learn anything.

Generally, we are so caught in the notion that our thinking is correct, that we eliminate all other possibilities. "We do this all the time," I think. Thây says that this *closed* mindset can be damaging; at its extreme, it leads to acts of violence.

Earlier today Thây said, "If your mind is pure, you will speak and act beautifully. If your mind is ugly, your speech and actions will bring about great suffering."

It is only day five of my journey, and already I have noticed that Thây does not wallow in dire messages as he teaches. He recognizes that there is suffering and he acknowledges the existence of happiness. These are facts. It is abundantly clear that he is interested in reducing pain and increasing joy. Earlier today, Thây had a number of us chuckling when he emphasized the necessity of non-attachment to one's view. He told a story of a renowned Buddhist teacher who said, "the Dharma Body is cow dung!" Essentially meaning: "Spiritual teachings are shit!" The famed Zen teacher had proclaimed this unusual dictum in order to shock people into understanding that even spiritual teachings are just a vehicle used to gain insight. Thây often says that teachings are like a boat. That boat should be used to take you across the river. Once on the other shore, if you pick that boat up and carry it, you will be weighed down unnecessarily. So, in order to deepen your whole view, you must be able to release it. That even includes your insight into Buddhism.

I think again about the possibility of shaving off my long, blonde hair.

Just before Thich Nhat Hanh began this monastic winter retreat here at Plum Village, he was teaching in India. Earlier this morning, during his talk, Thây reflected on the great Indian leader, Mahatma Gandhi, who once said, "In my process to find truth, I have discarded many ideas and learned many things." From that statement, Thây said it was evident that Gandhi had learned how to release his view. And that made him very wise.

I was delighted to hear Thây talk of Mahatma Gandhi, because I had recently met Gandhi's great-grandson, Rajmohan, while in Paris just before my pilgrimage. Rajmohan had been in France to promote his recent biography of his grandfather, and luckily, I had heard about it. In a bookstore in the Saint-Germain-des-Prés quarter, in a room so crowded that my seat was a stair, I sat on the edge, riveted by a fascinating talk. In fact, Rajmohan could have said anything and I would have been keen. I was just intensely happy to be in the same room with a direct relative of the masterful and legendary leader of peace.

During the question and answer period after Rajmohan had spoken, an audience member asked what Rajmohan hoped to achieve in his lifetime. Rajmohan stated that he hoped to be aware of and fight the injustices within himself so that he could fight injustice in the world as a whole.

That evening left an indelible mark on me in many unpredictable ways.

Afterward, as I walked back to my rented Paris apartment reflecting on Rajmohan's words, I began to feel queasy and a little sweaty. I guessed that the salmon I had eaten for dinner, the one that had looked so fresh at the local fish store, was probably tainted. I was right. I became deathly ill. Luckily, I managed to get home before succumbing to my stomach's full-on horror. Back in my apartment, in my isolated, ill, and fragile state, I felt incredibly vulnerable and entirely alone. But that vulnerability also unleashed a unique kind of courage. I remember thinking, "I just want to be kind."

On that long night, I pulled myself off the bathroom floor and up on to my feet. I turned on my computer and sent my entire email list the following message: "If I have sent you this email, it means that you are either my family, dear friend, casual friend, work colleague, someone I know a little bit, or even someone I have met just once . . . no matter, I want you to know that I think of you with kindness. May I be kind and thoughtful toward you always."

Thich Nhat Hanh had said earlier today that pain often brings insight—it opens your mind. There I was in glorious Paris, stricken with food poisoning on a lonely, grim night. Not pleasant at all. But I now see that my view had expanded that night. I had realized the importance of telling the people in my life that I cared deeply for them and hoped always to do so. I even sent that message to people I didn't like. And I emailed those who I thought might be a tad embarrassed by my outburst of raw emotion. In good health, I am much more cautious. I only wished that my parents had been alive to receive my message. They, of course, would have been the first to respond—in fact they would have expected a call from me if I were ill. That desolate night in France, my parents' absence intensified and the sick pit in my stomach plunged another story down. The next day, however, somewhat recovered from the attack of the contaminated fish, and after having sent my declaration of love email, I received loads of joyful responses and from the most unexpected of recipients. The dark cloud of despair lifted from over me. And a fresh braveness stirred within.

I realize now that meeting Gandhi's great-grandson, tinged with a bout of food poisoning, had caused a breakthrough that expanded my thinking and opened my mind—exactly what Thây had been talking about today. All of us have these "breakthrough opportunities" presented to us throughout our lives. But if we do not ground that experience somehow, it will leak away. Zen teacher Roshi Joan Sutherland describes it like this: "Without a way to deepen and broaden (that experience), to maintain a living relationship with it, it tends to fade into a fond or frustrating memory of what might have been."

In bed in my Hobbit-like monastic cave, just before falling asleep tonight, I have a memory from that night in Brazil. As the gun hung in mid-air, between life and death, attached to this adolescent's small hand, my focus had instantly sharpened, and I knew that I had absolutely no control. I was silent. Out of nervousness, or denial, or something, my boyfriend had blathered on, telling me later he thought that the gun wasn't loaded. I remember watching the young boy's trigger finger tense up in frustration while the atmosphere intensified. In the next moment of dead air, I shot a silent, strong look into my boyfriend's careless eyes, to signal my run. He immediately followed.

Never underestimate the possibility of a gun being loaded—this is the bit of wisdom I came away with.

Thich Nhat Hanh teaches *engaged* Buddhism, and he is the very definition of absorption and involvement with life. Thây dives deeply into complex situations with valor. To be in the world, experiencing it, and not off on the sidelines away from the action, builds a resilience as powerful as granite stone. A monk is not cavalier. But those who assume a monk renounces the world and lives in a nirvana-like dreamland do not know the life of a true monk.

⇜ Day 6 ⇝

Stopping:
The Message in the Ringing Bell

Plenty of people miss their share of happiness, not because they never found it, but because they didn't stop to enjoy it.
—WILLIAM FEATHER

The day my father was scheduled for triple bypass heart surgery, my two brothers and I were sitting in our Toronto homes unaware that our father was in a hospital bed in Ottawa. My father had forbidden my mother from telling us that he was about to have a potentially life-threatening surgery. Throughout most of his life, my dad worked pretty much non-stop. Up at 5:00 a.m. every day, he would work for a few hours before heading to the office. The rest of the family would rise to see work papers spread corner to corner across the dining room table, with my dad's nose buried deep in them. Returning home from the office well after the family had finished dinner, his evenings were more of the same—working at the dining room table. He also worked on weekends.

"If you live like you have lived in the last twenty years, it is clear, the most wonderful moment of your life will not arrive. Without the ability to stop, no insight can be attained."

Thich Nhat Hanh has just uttered this warning, which freaks me out—and he's not even here in person. This afternoon, I am watching a taped Dharma talk with a few of my fellow pilgrims in the meditation hall. "Our practice is "to be," not "to do." Learn to enjoy every moment of what you are doing." I gaze at Thây's image on the television screen. He is clearly saying that if we cannot stop, we cannot ever develop a deep understanding of life. Pausing leads to our ability to gain insight into our selves and the world. In Buddhist terms, this exploration is called *Vipashyana* and is much different than simply having an intellectual understanding of things. "We can only develop wisdom through experience." When the sage monk utters this bit of truth, it is another affirmation of the necessity of my journeying far from my geographical home, in order to add weight to my courage.

Earlier this morning, while pouring myself a cup of green tea, I saw a tall, lanky woman with a short crop of chestnut hair and wire glasses abruptly stop in the doorway in between the dining hall and the dishwashing area. It was a comical sight. She froze in the most awkward of rigid postures, clinging to the half open door for balance. She looked like a nervous squirrel trying to cross a road full of cars.

My fellow companion at New Hamlet was simply following a regular practice here. Whenever a bell rings—a gong or the telephone, or even the chimes in a church nearby—everyone stops. We are meant to focus on our breathing and stay silent and still for a few moments. I am getting used to this practice that initially seemed so strange to me. We just do not want to stop, like the stiff, lanky woman in the doorway, terror-stricken simply from having to stand still.

44

Buddhists love to talk about an ancient tale of a man on a galloping horse. In the story, because the horse is running so fast, it appears that the man on this mustang is going somewhere important. A person at the roadside shouts out to the man: "Where are you going?" The man on the speedy horse replies, "I don't know, ask the horse!" And if Zen tales aren't enough to remind us of the futility of our ways, philosophers drive the point home. Henry David Thoreau said, "The man whose horse trots a mile a minute does not carry the most important message."

Our culture has conditioned us to move at warp speed. A few years ago, I was visiting a friend in New York City. While walking to a SoHo brunch spot on an excruciatingly steamy afternoon in August, I found myself three paces behind my walking companion. Even at my speed, I was perspiring in the humidity. My friend turned around and said, very directly: "Mary, you're in New York City. You have to walk faster!" Never mind that she would be all sweaty for the rest of the day. My lovely friend—and I do love her—was accustomed to walking quickly simply from habit, as so many of us are in this modern world. If I lived in the City That Never Sleeps, I would most probably be trotting right along with the rest.

Before my pilgrimage, while in London and Paris, this is what I saw everyday: street after street of tense-faced, rail-thin people dressed in black, take-out coffee in one hand, mobile phone in the other, rushing—as if time were a blazing tyrant.

When Thây says that our habit energy is that runaway horse, I believe him.

Thây continues to enlighten this gathering of four pilgrims in the meditation hall, sitting like eager school children listening intently to the best of fairy tales—only these stories are true.

"Intellectually you know that life is beautiful, but it is impossible for you to get in touch with it because of your sorrow, anger, and fear. Therefore, you must free yourself from all of these cravings, jealousies, and projects . . . running after fame, power, and success . . . you will not be free."

In 2007, *Washington Post* columnist Gene Weingarten initiated a social experiment in Washington DC's Metro subway station.

On a cold January morning, a man sat in a metro station in Washington, DC and started to play the violin. He played six Bach pieces for about forty-five minutes. It was rush hour, when thousands of people went through the station, most of them on their way to work.

After three minutes, one middle-aged man noticed there was music playing. He slowed his pace and stopped for a few seconds, but then hurried away. A minute later, a woman threw a dollar in the till without stopping. Then, a man leaned against the wall to listen, but after a few moments looked at his watch and moved on. There was one person who paid attention—a three-year-old boy. But his mother tugged him along, even as the child turned his head back toward the musician the whole time. Several other children did the same. All their parents, without exception, forced them to move on.

In the forty-five minutes the musician played, only six people stopped and listened for a while. About twenty gave him money but didn't stop to listen. He collected $32. When he finished, no one noticed. No one applauded, and there was no recognition of any kind.

The musician was Joshua Bell, one of the finest violinists in the world. He played incredibly intricate Bach music on a violin worth 3.5 million dollars. Two days before his subway gig, Joshua Bell sold out a theater in Boston with seats averaging $100.

Joshua Bell playing incognito was part of a study that looked at perception, taste, and priorities of people. According to the *Washington Post*, the outlines of the experiment included the following questions: In a commonplace environment at an inappropriate hour, do we perceive beauty? Do we stop to appreciate it? Do we recognize talent in an unexpected context? If we are so rushed that we cannot recognize an exceptionally talented musician, playing some of the most intricate music ever written, how many other things are we missing?

The rest of Thây's taped Dharma talk today is about how we are all in a dream—we haven't woken up to the fact that we must "touch the present moment in order to find true peace and happiness." The root of Buddha is *Budd*, which means to wake up. I suppose that is one of the reasons there is walking meditation here at Plum Village. Thây teaches all of us *how* to walk. Today, through this television screen, Thich Nhat Hanh is explaining the proper way to approach this common activity:

> As you step, say to yourself, "I have arrived in the here and now." This is not a statement; it is a realization. You have been running your whole life and it has gotten you nowhere. Allow yourself to arrive—you must invest 100 percent in each step . . . to truly arrive. Put your mind in the sole of your foot, and then that step will become solid. Your foot is like the seal of an emperor on which it is written, "I have arrived."

Many days from now, I will hear Thây say this great thing again, in person.

This kind of contemplative walking on the monastery grounds has absolutely nothing in common with my speedy strides in New York City. And it looks very different from the coffee-wielding crew of grey faces I saw while in London and Paris. I wonder what those speedy Londoners would say if I were to stop them and suggest that they put their mind in the sole of their feet. They would look at me like I was a crazy person. Is this kind of walking even possible in a busy city? I take a moment to think about what happens when one walks with mindfulness.

Thich Nhat Hanh calls this kind of walking "walking like the Buddha." For a few days now, I have watched Thây carefully as he walks, and I see that his movements have a different quality than mine. His steps are careful but firm. They are even and continuous. And they are slow. My steps are thoughtless. They are uneven and arrhythmic. And I always want to go faster than the group—always. But there are moments when I have glimpses of flow. During those precious seconds, I feel time stand still. Thây calls that kind of experience being deeply in the present moment. During these rare occasions, I feel glorious. I am free from worrying about the past, and I am not obsessively planning the future. And importantly, I am not disconnected from myself. My mind and body are together.

These insightful instances are not accessible through swift and sweaty NYC strides. But when I am able to slow down and "touch the moment," as Thây says, I simply feel better, lighter, and more alive. I notice what is happening around me. I see the plum trees. I smell the wet grass. I hear the songs of the wrens. I feel wafts of cool air on my face. It is strange to think that most of the time I really don't see, smell, hear, or feel things around me—not like I do here, anyway. And maybe that's part of living in a big city. Maybe we don't want to admit that we live on cement streets with hydro wires canopying our heads. Perhaps that's why we go into sensation-numbing overdrive.

By today, my sixth day, I have become quite fond of the chiming bells. I think of the panic-stricken woman who I had spied this morning, stuck between two rooms. It's her first day here. Maybe after a few days, she will relax. Now, I like these pauses. The *stopping* allows me to check in with myself. Perhaps I am breathing poorly or speaking incorrectly to someone. I've noticed this *pausing* causes me to reflect, and if necessary, adjust my behavior. When that bell rings, it brings me into a useful, contemplative place. Even though this ceasing of movement still feels rather odd, I am beginning to see its usefulness in developing what Thich Nhat Hanh calls *shamatha*, or *stopping*—an immensely important aspect of meditation.

Did I have to go to a far-away monastery across an ocean to take in the scent of leaves on the moist earth? Here, in the French countryside, natural beauty surrounds me. One step out of the residence and I am encircled by rolling hills of red apple and plum trees, masses of entwined grapevines, and golden brown sunflowers. Gorgeous. This environment commands me to pay attention, causing all of my senses to pique. I become aware of everything around me, and my place within that beauty. Why don't I do this at home?

⚜

Memories of my workaholic father walk with me on the wet grass of New Hamlet. My mother did end up convincing my father of the importance of letting my two brothers and I know of his heart surgery before he was to have his ribs cracked open. That day, the three of us traveled to an Ottawa Hospital and saw our father come through the operation just fine. And even though my dad had already taken an early retirement a few years back, after my mother's cancer diagnosis, a triple bypass made him face his own mortality. The health scare compelled my father to spend more quality time with the whole family.

When Thây says, "Walk like a Buddha, like a free person," I think of my dad. What would life have been like if my father had kept up his excessive work? In this over-caffeinated, overwhelming, over-everything world of ours, I wonder if we will understand how to work with greater intelligence and ease before some illness demands that we stop.

☞ Day 7 ☜

Effort:
How *Not* To Become Superwoman

*Maintain your health. Be joyful. Do not force yourself to
do things you cannot do.*

—THE BUDDHA

Yesterday the Sisters of New Hamlet put silver bangles
on the wrist bones of the skeleton that stands at the
back of the meditation hall. Yes, there are human bones
hanging with the Buddha. I am quietly reading *The Maha
Prajna Paramita Heart Sutra* (the Buddha's teachings on
the great path for the perfection of wisdom), when I
look up to see three giggling nuns placing a bejeweled
bony hand onto a bare hip. The nun's magnetic laughter
draws me to them. As I approach three very alive beings,
laughing and playing with one ancient relic, the beautiful
strangeness of the scene hits me. Glumness is the more
common demeanor around reminders of death. But these
Sisters are jubilant.

I ask the jolliest of the lot why a human skeleton is
in the meditation hall. Through more giggles, the Sister

with the beaming smile replies that *she* is there simply to remind everyone about their posture—spying straight bones, apparently, keeps some people from slouching. A second answer comes from the same nun: "The skeleton is here as a reminder of your death." Yes, she was referring to *my* death.

Whenever I gaze at the smooth, white skull of my skeletal meditation companion, I remember that I am going to die. The Sisters of New Hamlet, the ones who have decorated these bones, treat this quiet presence as if she is a cherished child whom they are adorning and admiring. I now see that in their behavior is their wise reverence of death.

I sometimes think of the nuns as mischievous elves of the all-knowing monk who is Thich Nhat Hanh. And they are all in this together, weaving their communal magic—the alchemy that supports my journey of awakening here. It's as if the nuns understand why I have come to Plum Village. They seem to know that my parents are no longer on earth to support and love me. The Sisters are aware of my needs, yet they have never asked any personal questions. These intuitive creatures transcend the usual bounds of relating. They leap over silly, meaningless queries as if playing a joyful game of hopscotch.

I think of how, in the West, one of the first questions one asks upon meeting a new person is, "What do you do?" Here at the monastery, instead of being spoken *to*, you are more likely to be spoken *with*. Countless times, some mysteriously gifted nun has approached me and proclaimed something obvious, compelling me to look more deeply into the "obvious." Yesterday a Vietnamese nun announced, "Mary, look at the cerulean sky; it is so big and full of life!" In French, it sounded even more joyous, and yes, she said "cerulean." I wonder if the sky-loving nun realized that her words immediately banished thoughts of my parental loss. I wonder if all the Sisters of New Hamlet realize the depth of their supportive role

in my quest to take refuge and anchor myself to my true
Home within.

Later today, I venture into town to do laundry and
errands, a privilege we are allowed once a week on lazy
days when no particular meditations or studies are scheduled. These are days to engage in activities of your liking—reading, socializing, or getting some chores done.
On this casual afternoon, I am sitting in the one and only
internet cafe in a quaint French village, reading an email
from a friend of mine in Toronto. I only half-jokingly call
her superwoman. My energetic friend is married with four
children all under the age of eight, two golden retrievers,
and a wild orange cat, *and* she has a demanding full-time
job. Her house is enormous, she does all the cleaning and
cooking, and to top it off, her home has been under reno-
vation for well over a year. In her message, she says that
her office work has recently become particularly demanding, and now that it's holiday season she has been to five
parties in a row, with too much wine and rich food. She
admits that she is in dire need of an alcohol-free night
soon. In a few days she will be hosting forty-five people
(45!) at her home for a sit-down dinner and then the
following week, another thirty guests for the same. She is
exhausted.

Only yesterday, Thây talked about a modern kind of
sickness in which we work with the wrong *kind* of effort.
I will hear him say this many times during my pilgrimage—that we often labor our bodies and minds too hard
and become carried away with the goal of completing
our projects and managing our social schedules. This is
the cause of much of our suffering and ill health. As I
read the email from my friend, I reflect on Thây's revelation. And I understand that a unique kind of mindful
intelligence is essential while working, so that no harm

comes to the body or mind. If we exhaust our resources over and over again, as many of us clearly do, eventually, the well will dry up.

I sit back on a creaky chair, gazing at a computer screen juxtaposed by an ancient mahogany desk and the silver-haired French proprietor reading Flaubert in the corner. More of Thây's words fill my mind: "This tension blocks the blossoming of our peace—we are pushing and forcing, and just simply overdoing things." Thây had used the example of a string on a musical instrument to shed light on Right Effort. If the string is too loose, when you pluck it, there will be no sound, but if the string is too taut, it will break when played. And there it is—how does one walk the middle line between laziness and over-exertion, between austere asceticism and overindulgence?

I pack up my computer, pay two Euros to the Flaubert-reading gentleman, and offer him my French thank you.

"Decide to be free. Decide to be free. Decide to be free." Thây's wise words are rolling over and over in my head as I walk back home from the village to New Hamlet. What am I doing? Am I filling my time with too many tasks and projects, tiring myself out with an excess of social gatherings? When I'm overloaded, it is impossible to be mindful. I do not want to break myself down. I do not want my friends, the friends whom I love, to become ill from overexertion. To work with joy and ease toward the things that truly matter—that is how to thrive.

Thich Nhat Hanh's relaxed presence is remarkable, and yet I know that he has accomplished difficult feats in his life. And that takes effort. It is no simple task to become a Zen Buddhist master, let alone a human rights activist or an author of over one hundred book. Thây is also the founder of many monasteries and social service organizations, all the while maintaining a busy teaching schedule around the world. Have I mentioned that this sprightly figure is eighty-four years old?

I wonder what it is about the way this graceful monk works that gives him this outstanding capacity to pro-duce greatness, and all the while maintain his health. Yesterday, as I listened to Thây speak about this modern sickness of pushing ourselves sometimes to the point of illness just to accomplish our goals, I became transfixed watching him drink tea. In one movement, the careful monk had cradled his ceramic, handle-free cup and swept it smoothly toward his wise mouth. I looked at his face as he took a sip—the monk *knew* he was drinking; his face was full of peace. Thây then gently placed the vessel down. There was absolutely nothing hurried about any of these movements. And yet, I couldn't help but think of the formidable effort that must have been required for Thich Nhat Hanh to complete his projects. Thây does not rush. Witnessing this lucid monk's relaxed yet exceedingly productive manner helped me to realize that success comes from a mastery of Right Effort, an essen-tial step on the Noble Eightfold Path. I notice that Thây works gracefully with ease in a way that must not exhaust his resources; then the spry octogenarian directs those efforts toward cultivating evermore wisdom and enlight-ening the world.

Earlier this morning, as I meditated with the bejew-eled skeleton, I noticed the bald monastic heads of the Sisters more than usual. And it made me think of skulls and death. Is that the modest, yet brazen reason for strip-ping away hair—to see that bony skull—to remind one of the closeness of the grave? I remember the crypt of Capu-chin monks in Rome where there are piles of human skulls next to a sign that reads, *We are as you once were. You will be as we are. A memento mori.* I had read about this reminder of death in *How Shakespeare Changed Everything* by Stephen Marche. Have the bald monks understood death? These thoughts spin around in my mind as I walk back to the monastery from the village, and the musings stay with me all the way through dinner.

After dinner and silence finishes, I tell a Dutch friend at the table that I'm thinking of shaving my head. She looks straight at me and says that I am not permitted to engage in this Buddhist ritual. "Only monastics have this privilege. Head shaving happens during the ordination ceremony. Do you want to take vows and become a nun?" I have a moment of disappointment mixed with relief as I take in my new realization. "I get to keep my hair."

Tonight I am lying in bed, running my hands through my hair, and thinking of all the people I know who work to extremes, with the kind of exertion that is destroying them. And not only that—some of them pursue *questionable* goals, sinking their lives into making money, or gaining power, or seeking fame for its own sake. I think of the times I myself have bulldozed through life, in pursuit of fleeting pleasures. The nuns do not waste time on these transient pursuits many of us damage our health by running after. Instead, they aspire to perfect the Buddha's teaching on Right Effort, to live a life that is physically, emotionally, and mentally invigorating *and* balanced. I imagine a robed Vietnamese nun on a Paris street, with a takeout coffee in one hand, a mobile phone in the other, and a cigarette dangling from her mouth, rushing to get somewhere. I smile at the absurdity of that picture. It seems the levelheaded Sisters are rubbing off on me.

☞ Day 8 ☜

Silence:
How *Not* To Build a Fire

If a person can be gracious and courteous to strangers, it shows she is a citizen of the world and that her heart is no island cut off from other lands, but a continent that joins them.

—Francis Bacon

A few days ago, I noticed that a fire hadn't been started in the dining hall fireplace, and many shivering nuns and pilgrims were already lined up for breakfast. And I must say, November mornings in a drafty French monastery are chilly, to put it mildly. The nuns were busy cooking gigantic pots of oatmeal, so I asked if I was allowed to make a fire. I was indeed—anyone was— and it turned out that my Sisters appreciated the fire-making help.

One of my favorite things to do is make a fire. I love everything about it—gathering the kindling, placing the wood just right, and then watching the flames build. So, on most days I go downstairs to the dining hall before breakfast and happily build my little fire.

Every morning, until after breakfast, there is a period of "noble silence," which means there is no talking allowed during any activity, let alone the making of any fires. Sitting on the wooden bench at the fireside, I follow my usual routine and start planning my log piling strategy. As soon as I place crumpled paper perfectly under a log, I feel a stream of hot breath down my neck. I look over my shoulder and into the light blue eyes of an older French woman with silver hair and a flourish of color round her neck. She is so close to me that her stylish crimson and olive scarf brushes against my left cheek. She must be new here. I don't recognize her. This chic-looking Frenchwoman silently gestures to me about something I'm not quite sure of. I continue building my fire.

Buddhists have long practiced this tradition of engaging in periods of noble silence or quietude. The Buddha was known to remain silent if a question was posed to him from someone who was not in a position to understand the answer, or if the question itself was wrongly put in the first place. On several occasions, the Buddha had carefully explained that language was limited and could not describe the *Ultimate Truth*. Whenever the Buddha remained silent in this way, it was called noble silence. Years ago, during my first silent retreat in India, having not uttered a word for ten days, I realized both the limitations and the power of language. For weeks afterward, I became highly cognizant of every single word that left my mouth, and my responsibility for the meaning of it all. The experience was liberating and empowering.

There is, however, a humorous side to this Buddhist ritual. Some people feel compelled to communicate in other ways, like, for instance, mouthing words, whispering loudly, or creating somewhat frantic hand gestures, as in a silly game of charades. Just such a comical episode

57

is happening now. The Frenchwoman breathing down my neck thinks I am making this fire poorly—that I can tell by the way she is shaking her head, exhaling in great sighs, and zealously gesturing for me to move aside. She wants to take my prized seat as head fire-maker, and I am insulted. This is what she is trying to tell me in the heavy silence. My frustration mounts as she picks up my carefully laid log and it falls flat. "No air can get under that log—you need air for fire!" But I can't say this aloud. I'm not able to say anything, and this woman is blatantly belittling my fire-building skills. She thinks she knows better than me, and that's just not true. I try not to feel annoyed, but the emotion seizes me. Here in the deafening silence, I can't say a word. I should not react, but I already have.

Before Thich Nhat Hanh's Dharma talks, a nun or monk will remind us of our neurotic tendencies by petitioning aloud: "May we be relieved of our superiority complexes, inferiority complexes, and also equality complexes." The first time I heard this appeal, I got stumped on the "equality" part. So, today, after recognizing my own superiority complex and that of the French fire-dictator, I turned my mind toward equality complexes.

In our modern society, the term *equality* most often represents a pinnacle to be reached. I have always thought of equal human rights, for example, as a highly valued ideal. Now the monks have me thinking, again, about yet another conditioned way of viewing the world.

Equality is a "complex," from the Buddhist perspective, because, as with the complexes of superiority and inferiority, an equality complex involves comparisons. Because we have the wrong view of ourselves, we have the tendency to compare ourselves with other selves—"I am as good a fire-maker as she," for example. Comparisons pose problems because they discount the truth that *we are in each other*. Again, because all of us contain the same elements of the world, any comparison is not existentially relevant. Since all of us are made up of things that we are not—water, minerals, oxygen, that coffee you just drank, the green tea I just sipped, *I am in you, and you are in me*. The French dictator is in me; I am in the French dictator. You and me and the French dictator all contain the same non-human elements. According to Buddhism, if we do not see this truth, then we have a complex. We would be discriminating.

But let me get back to my complex, "Who is the more highly skilled fire-maker?" Today, I have not understood the wisdom of non-discrimination. I am actively discriminating against my fellow pilgrim, as she seems to be doing with me. It is clear that there is no real communication possible while discrimination is present. And even though silence seems to communicate in a myriad of ways—the cold shoulder of anger and hostility, shunning, ignoring, the silence of incomprehension or confusion, the passivity of passive-aggressive behavior—none of this is *true* communication. The French dictator and I are not communicating with each other here, in this silence. Neither of us have the wisdom of non-discrimination.

Earlier in the week, Thây had illuminated this teaching of non-discrimination by telling a story of a time in which he had been holding a nail in his left hand and a hammer in his right. When he went to hit the nail with the hammer, he mistakenly hammered his left hand. Thây then asked us: "Did my right hand scold my left hand for being in the way? No. My right hand immediately held and soothed my left hand. My right hand had the wisdom of non-discrimination."

Mythologist and writer Joseph Campbell, in a book of conversations with Michael Toms, described a teaching from the nineteenth-century Indian mystic Sri Ramakrishna. "Insofar as you identify yourself with the consciousness that moves and lives in your body, you've identified with that which you share with me."

His Holiness the Dalai Lama says this: "There is a common consciousness which is our ground and so in consciousness, we are one."

And it all comes back to the question of how to be comfortable with the fact that this consciousness that is within me is the same universal consciousness that is in this bossy dictator. How do I develop the wisdom of non-discrimination?

Of course, all of us have unique capacities on the "outside"—a seven-foot-tall basketball player can dunk a ball in a hoop, whereas the five-foot four-inch French farmer next door to me here cannot. But internally, the NBA star and the farmer contain the same non-human elements and the same spiritual potential. Inside, of course, we are all the same.

Somehow, between two silently battling pilgrims, a full fire managed to come to life. As I line up for breakfast, I think about how the silence had revealed the quickness and futility of my negative reaction to something outside of myself. I don't have to allow myself to be yanked from my inner foundation. And not only that, without the annoying French dictator to challenge me, I wouldn't have had the chance to toughen up and connect with that rock-solid part of myself. What is that old saying about our enemies being our best teachers? I think that's true.

☞ Day 9 ☜

Action:
Why Saving a Bunch of
Ants Is Good

Man is the sum of all his actions.

—JEAN PAUL SARTRE

Some years ago, I was on a canoe trip in a remote lake district of Northern Ontario with a great boyfriend named Doug and two of his friends. One night, the four of us found ourselves a tad desperate in search of a suitable campsite before sundown. One of the last sites available had been overrun with masses of black ants all convened in probably the most gigantic anthill known to man. If anyone else had been around, they would have seen four very tired campers, paddles in hand, staring dumbstruck at an imposing colony of crawling bugs. Silence finally broke when Doug's friend announced that we should pour lighter fluid on the bug hill and set the ants aflame. To say I was horrified at the thought of burning down the ants' home, menacing as it was, would be an understatement.

I turned to Doug and said that I was not about to be part of any ant-burning posse. Doug heartily agreed.

Karma simply means "action" and is of three kinds: thought, speech, and bodily action. Your thoughts have power, your words have power, and your bodily actions have power. Everything you think, say, and do will produce a chain of action and reaction with infinite and unknowable consequences. You cannot take back ugly behavior. In his book *Buddha Mind, Buddha Body*, Thây emphasizes that there is no escape: "Your not-so-beautiful behavior has immediately gone out ahead into the future and begun the chain of action and reaction."

It may seem insignificant to burn a pile of ants, but in fact this kind of thing is done every single day because humans are so very often shortsighted and selfish. This erroneous thinking has led to destruction and environmental imbalance, as the renowned entomologist E.O. Wilson warned: "If insects were to vanish, the terrestrial environment would soon collapse into chaos . . . " Apparently, ants move more earth than earthworms, making them essential for soil. And of course we need the soil renewed for flowers and plants to survive, but if protecting the vegetation we eat is not enough of an incentive to watch our actions, there's always this Buddhist parable, which I came across many years after bearing witness to the ants.

There once was an old monk who, through diligent practice, had attained a certain degree of spiritual penetration. This monk had a young eight-year-old novice. One day the monk looked at the boy's face and saw that the boy would die within the next few months. Saddened by this, the monk told the boy to take a long holiday and go visit his parents. "Take your time," said the monk. "Don't hurry back." For he felt the boy should be with his family when he died. Three months later, to the monk's astonishment, he saw the boy walking back up the mountain. When the boy arrived, the monk looked intently at his face and saw that the boy would now live to a ripe old age. "Tell me everything that happened while you were away," said the monk. The boy told of his journey down the mountain, of villages he passed through, of river fords and mountains he climbed. Then the boy told the monk of how one day he came upon a flooded stream. As the boy tried to cross the flowing stream, he noticed that a colony of ants had become trapped on a small island formed by the flood. Moved by compassion for these poor creatures, the boy took a tree branch and laid it across one part of the stream until it touched the little island. As the ants made their way across, the boy held the branch steady, until he was sure all the ants had escaped to dry land.

"So," thought the old monk, "that is why the gods have lengthened his days."

In his book *The Art of Power*, Thich Nhat Hanh emphasizes that "The quality of your action depends on the quality of your being." If you yourself are not happy, for example, it is impossible to offer true happiness to any other being. "So, there is a link between doing and being. If you don't succeed in being, you can't succeed in doing."

❧ ☙

I am sitting in the Dharma Hall of Upper Hamlet listening to Thich Nhat Hanh explain that it is possible to neutralize the karma you have generated. Thây is describing how *mindfulness* can embrace an unwholesome action in order to neutralize its effects, and that same mindfulness can also initiate some kind of wholesome action. So there may have been a way out for that band of near-reckless campers all those years ago, even if they had been cavalier enough to burn a bunch of ants.

Before relaying the following grim event from the Vietnam War, Thây says, "Not only does mindfulness heal the present—it heals the past and the future."

Years after the Vietnam War, Thich Nhat Hanh organized meditation retreats for U.S. war veterans. On one of those retreats, there had been an extremely traumatized ex-soldier. This veteran had unintentionally contributed to the deaths of five Vietnamese children during the war. The American soldier's unit had been destroyed by Vietnamese guerillas, causing the deaths of many of the soldier's co-combatants. In his grief and anger, the soldier had sought retaliation for the deaths. He inserted explosives into sandwiches and then planted the toxic food where those same Vietnamese soldiers would find and eat them. Instead of the soldiers finding the poisoned sandwiches, though, five young Vietnamese children did. Upon witnessing the terrible scene, the U.S. soldier was filled with dread. He knew there was no way to save the innocent children. The hospital was miles away. Those children had died an agonizing death.

The American war veteran had lived a life of tortured guilt for many years afterward. Thây tells us now that before the war veteran relayed his story to Thây, he hadn't told anyone of it, except his mother, and she hadn't been able to relieve his guilt. After the war, any time the ex-soldier found himself around children, his suffering became immense. He couldn't manage to be in the presence of any child, so strong was his remorse and pain.

Thây went on to explain that, upon hearing of the five children's deaths from the war veteran, he had told the veteran that the children's deaths had not been a good thing. That karma was not good. But it was possible for this soldier to do something else—something good to neutralize that bad action of his past. Thich Nhat Hanh reminded the veteran that every day, children were dying in many countries, and for simple reasons such as the lack of one tablet of medicine. Thây told the war veteran that it was possible for him to do something now. This ex-soldier could choose to save the lives of five other children. Not only that, but he could also save the lives of more than five children. If this truly regretful man could do that for some time, it would neutralize the karma, the destructive action of the past. Thây tells us that within minutes of counseling the war veteran, all those years ago, that wounded soldier leapt out of his negative state of mind. He immediately aspired to help the dying children of the world. Thây says that the remorseful ex-soldier, newly invigorated, went on to actively save the lives of countless children in the world—children who would have certainly died otherwise.

The ex-soldier's elevated act in the present transformed his destructive act of the past; catapulted him out of guilt, sadness, and regret; and created his immensely rewarding and peaceful future. In his book, *Buddha Mind, Buddha Body*, Thich Nhat Hanh writes: "Everything is impermanent—your guilt, your anger, your fear. Things can transform very quickly, if you know the practice."

His Holiness the Dalai Lama, in his book *Path to Bliss*, writes that "Some people misunderstand the concept of karma. They take the Buddha's doctrine of the law of causality to mean that all is pre-determined, that there is nothing that the individual can do. This is a total misunderstanding. The very term karma or action is a term of active force, which indicates that future events are within your own hands. Since action is a phenomenon that is committed by a person, a living being, it is within your own hands whether or not you engage in action."

Even if we've made the most gruesome of human mistakes, there is still a way out. The teachings of the Buddha help us understand that we have the ability to neutralize our negative karma and elevate our actions in the present. Each day we have the opportunity to save and protect the lives of many beings in the world. Acting on that power brings immense joy.

65

⟅ Day 10 ⟆

Patience:
How to Skin a Nut

Do not cut what you can untie.

—JOSEPH JOUBERT

The 5:00 a.m. gong has just rung. I half wake up to feel the cold air on my nose again. For the tenth time, I resist getting up. For the tenth time, I do not want to emerge from underneath my warm blanket. And for the tenth time, I do manage to get up and out of bed on time. As usual, the morning practice will start at 5:30 a.m., so I wrap my ivory wool shawl around my chilly body and head down the residence stairs toward the Buddha Hall, making my usual washroom pit stop on my way.

Bleary-eyed, padding down this dark, monastic stairwell, I feel both comforted by the familiar activity and anxious because of the routine. But this challenge of rising on cold, black mornings, day after tough day, is building my character—I can feel it. Somewhat optimistically, I am buoyed by the thought as I head toward the Buddha Hall.

I take my regular pause at the tea station, tepid water my only choice of beverage until the boilers are lit post-meditation. I take a sip of the bland drink and contemplate repetitive behaviors. Even if I enjoy a routine, often, when I have recognized some patterned behavior in myself, I have changed the approach out of fear of establishing a habit that will become difficult to break. Of course, some fixations are dead simple to crack, like waking up early, for example. "Is there anyone who loves rising before dawn every day?" I wonder. As I set my half-drunk cup of water down, I remember that one definitely needs to carve away at oneself, in order to sculpt a strong structure. Today, as I walk before dawn toward the Buddha, my strict ballet training comes to mind. That dancer's discipline had set me for life in many useful ways. So, I know that there is value in this getting up early business, but I have never managed to consistently master it.

I do, however, always love the first moment I step into the captivating meditation hall—with its Buddhist intrigue, vaulted ceiling, walls of grey stone, and ancient chestnut-colored wooden beams. This morning, the gleaming statue of the Buddha gazes back at me for the tenth glorious time—the eyes of that omniscient mind. The Buddha's breathtaking majesty is a stabilizing presence. I take my seat, this time in the second row near the back, and gaze at the conformity of the muddy brown monastic robes in the room. Shaved female heads are either covered with brown wool caps or naked, shining in the light although some have a five o'clock shadow that makes these radiant Zen Buddhist nuns appear mortal. The magnificent heads are perched on perfectly erect Buddha spines—the eyes on these heads don't dart around like those of the rest of us here. At 5:30 a.m., on the dot, the meditation practice begins. There are bells, chants, guided instructions, and slow mindful walking in an oblong circle around the rows of meditation seats, plus our regular practice of *bowing to the earth*—prostrations toward the resolute Buddha. Today, I am instructed to "breathe in the stream in the forest, and smile as I breathe out with the stream in the forest." This morning's practice, as usual, is one hour and a half in length. I manage to feel inspired by the meditation routine today, but then a thought sneaks into my mind: "What if I were to do this every single day of my life?" The thought terrifies me. As I walk out of the hall, I again stare at the conformity of the brown-robed Sisters.

After a brief rest in my room, lying flat on my back to stretch out post-meditation, I make my way down to the dining hall. It's 8:00 and time for breakfast. I serve myself the usual—an orange, oatmeal with brown sugar, hot soy milk, and almonds—routine again—and then quietly choose a seat across from one of my Irish/French friends, a woman I like very much. Of course, there is no talking during meals. It's easy to notice what people near us are doing, though. And in the silence, I catch sight of my friend deeply concentrated on the same task I am immersed in—the fine art of methodically peeling the skins off of several almonds. My hands are sticky from the orange I just ate, so removing the peel from these little gems proves to be a bit of a challenge. My friend is struggling, too.

One by one, our Sisters and friends leave the dining hall, happily sated from their breakfast. Soon there is just my friend and I, sitting across from one another and still stripping the skins off the nuts. At home, I would never, ever sit with an almond for twenty minutes—I just wouldn't spend my time doing that. But here, something interesting happens. As I patiently uncover the slippery nuts, I feel surprisingly connected to my friend in our communal act—like we silently understand each other. Not that we are both peeling almonds—that's ordinary—but that the act is causing something else to build within us. We sit in reverence here. We silently applaud the other's tenacity and patience. I can feel this in our unified presence. After the silent meal, I look up at my friend. There is no one else left in the dining hall except the two of us. I smile. The face across from me glows.

Later on, I reflect on this morning's almond breakfast. "Our capacity to endure waiting affects every part of our lives," I realize. With patience on our side, we will stay the course when times are turbulent.

Since I left my home in Canada, my strength of mind has been building. Many times, while alone in France before my pilgrimage began, I had often felt lonely—the desolation that comes from being geographically distant from every single person that you love. But I knew that somehow, if I could be patient, my life would change for the better. Thây says, "Like a garden, the seeds we plant in our lives need time to grow." The capable monk says that all we have to do is water and love these planted seeds, and time and space will work their magic.

After ten days of slow-paced monastery life, one thing I know is that I do not want to get on a runaway horse and speed through life. The tense-faced, mobile-phone/coffee/cigarette–wielding Parisians and Londoners I saw before my pilgrimage began drove that point home. I would watch those urbanites carelessly tossing their daring unfiltered Gauloises on ancient European cobblestones—not the romantic Paris I love. Here, in Plum Village, I realize the possibility of soothing my sore soul slowly and firmly. Countless days of tethering my mind to the practice of meditation and patience-building ordinary tasks like "nut peeling" are the balm for my aches.

I have to admit that after returning home from my pilgrimage, I haven't kept company with almonds for twenty minutes, but on one day, I spent ten minutes with a small handful. It felt like an eternity, but it reminded me of the immense value of patience. The discipline of patience is my best friend. She deserves an honorable seat in my Home within. Having the fortitude to wisely endure waiting changes everything for the better. Storms have a beginning and end. It seems to me now that patience is often all that's needed to ride out those days of thunder.

Day 11

Joy:
Cooking with the Boys

*Grief can take care of itself, but to get the full value of joy,
you must have somebody to divide it with.*

—MARK TWAIN

"Alright then, who wants to help cook lunch?" My
savior has arrived. The redeemer comes in the form
of a man who looks to be in his late twenties, with tousled
brown hair, glasses, a sweet-looking face, and a rolling
Scottish accent that awakens memories of my beloved
Glaswegian father.

I am sitting with several pilgrims on the bare floor in
a drafty room at Upper Hamlet, the monks' residences.
We are gathering to have a discussion about Thây's talk
from earlier this morning. These discourses are meant to
examine the teachings of the day, but sometimes they
stray off course, and pilgrims gab about unrelated personal issues. I lose my patience whenever a discussion
wades into self-indulgent, therapy-like territory that is
off-topic. I look around the room. Across from me sits

the dark-haired Italian guy, the object of a small, fleeting crush that instantly evaporated when he said something stupid. Beside him sits the young American Tom. I always enjoy what Tom has to say. Next to him sits a rough and tough muscle-bound Newfoundlander with tattoos, along with a few others. I'm cold, as usual, have no proper cushion to sit on, and some of the faces here seem a tad droopy. I want out.

The man seeking help in the kitchen is a pleasant young Scot named Stuart. The Scot hasn't even finished his sentence when my hand shoots straight up, seemingly before my mind directs it. "I'll do it!" I have volunteered. "Lovely, then." Stuart gives me a big smile and tells me to follow him. The next minute, I am in a large kitchen—a whole house of gigantic pots and ladles. I feel instantly happy.

When you cook, you cook. When you wash dishes, you wash dishes. When you eat, you simply eat—period. That is the path to happiness, so says the Buddha.

The tattooed Newfoundlander has also volunteered to be part of the lunch-making crew, along with three other men. I am the sole woman. Next thing I know, I am being instructed to chop a mountain of carrots beside the Newfoundlander. A large anchor stares at me from a muscled arm. And then the flirting begins. But it's harmless, and we've got ocean-size batches of soup to brew on a strict time schedule. And besides, the boy from *The Rock* is brutally honest and endearingly funny.

I have now chopped exactly six carrots, and there are probably a hundred more to go, but somehow this doesn't feel like a chore. I think about why that is. We are social creatures, all of us, and we need company—we thrive on it. But if we are to enjoy our time together, our comrades must be somewhat like-minded associates. I feel that here. Even though each one of us in this soup-concocting crew is unique and from varying backgrounds and countries, all of us share a common interest. Broadly,

71

that is a serious curiosity surrounding the teachings of the Buddha, and specifically, about those of Thich Nhat Hanh. Even though our life situations are mysterious to each other, they have compelled us to venture here, far from our homes and easy lifestyles and into this kitchen monastery, where bunches of rosemary herbs live. And that is why I can scrub these orange vegetables with enthusiasm, and slice them with joy. A chore that would normally daunt me transforms into one of ease because of my community of soup-making, Buddhist-loving, adventure-seeking brothers here. There is an unspoken understanding and respect we share for one another. That is immensely uplifting.

The Scot has full control over the kitchen. We are Stuart's obedient and joyful workers, and the food will be delicious because of it. The tattoos start singing some kind of Celtic ditty. It's catchy and all of us hum along. Humming and cooking—it's a breeze for me to feel joyous.

I think about the sorry souls still up in that cold monastic room, trying to make sense of life and all their suffering. Sometimes, it is just better to get out of your head and move—do something, anything. I feel this very strongly now, here in the kitchen, happily concocting potions with the boys.

Thich Nhat Hanh says that it is possible to feel happy no matter what our circumstances. The optimistic monk says that we just need to know how to navigate the terrain. In the morning talk today, Thây used the example of a thorny rose: "If we want to pick a rose, we have to touch some thorns. So, we must find a way to understand the thorns that are there with the rose. Our negative feelings are like those thorns. Thorns inevitably exist with the petals of a rose and those beautiful petals are like our joy. So, we must not think that we can't be happy because there are some thorns around. The rose petals are still there." Thây explained that we can have a *thorn* of sadness in our heart, for example, but still be able to experience the *flower* of joy. The more we practice this way of living, the more joyful we become, no matter what the situation. And this is vital, because joy is a factor of enlightenment.

"Breathing in, I feel joy. Breathing out, I feel joyful." Thây taught us this meditation to nourish our joy, to encourage us to let go of that which makes us tired, sad, or worried. Without joy, the Buddha said, one cannot become liberated.

The Newfoundlander is still singing the Celtic ditty.

I wonder if the pilgrims discussing Thây's talk right now up in that bleak, cold residence are wading into poor-me territory as they complain about their various sorrows. Are they using the group discussion as a vehicle to announce their personal unrest in the world, rather than examine the Buddha's teachings? Yes, I am cynically scoffing at my fellow pilgrims. This is not kind of me. But there it is. I look over at Stuart. With a gleaming knife, the Scot is whole-heartedly chopping a big bush of thyme for the soup. The young chef is entirely immersed in this everyday task. And I also know that Stuart has had a lot of painful situations in his family. Yet there is no complaining or carrying on about his problems. In forty days, I will never hear Stuart utter one negative word—ever. He simply gets on with it. He gives and gives, orchestrating these massive culinary creations that foster joy.

Stuart is masterfully building a wise connection to his Home within—that is clear—and it's an inspiring sight that nourishes my resolve as I furnish my glorious Home. I love Stuart for his quiet integrity, commitment, and abiding influence on me.

↫ Day 12 ↬

Humility:
Brazil Against Germany

Blessed are the meek for they shall inherit the earth.

—MATTHEW 5:5

In the residence of New Hamlet, a nasty argument is escalating between two visiting women. The players: Rita, a forthright Brazilian with flaming red hair and facial features as strong as her opinions, and Angelika, a pale and quiet German with beige hair, beige skin, and beige eyes. Even her dress, stockings, and shoes are camel-colored, making her seem all the more like a soft, wounded puppy.

It was never going to turn out well.

This morning after breakfast, the three of us happen to be in the washing area together. I am quietly brushing my teeth at the sink when I hear the two pilgrims begin to bicker a few feet to my right. There seems to be some kind of disagreement over a travel arrangement. I gather that there is only one place left in the car that is going to the village, and both of them want that seat. It seems that feisty Rita is attempting to maneuver her way into the treasured spot, which has already been given to Angelika. Finally worn down from Rita's relentless pleas, an obviously annoyed but still puppyish Angelika tells Rita that she can go ahead and take the seat since she has been complaining about it so much. The Brazilian gets angry. She is clearly up for a fight. But the frail German will have none of it—she gives the feisty one the silent treatment. This only infuriates Rita. She says that she is Brazilian and likes to speak her mind, that her "heated" way of talking is simply how she communicates, and she means no offense. This makes the reserved German clam up even more. And on and on it goes. Rita keeps provoking Angelika, causing the quiet girl to retreat even further. The Brazilian demands that Angelika bare her soul and speak her mind, while the wounded German can't seem to bear the thought of revealing any true emotions to this demanding stranger. Meanwhile, I cringe at the corner sink, my mouth full of toothpaste. It is an excruciating scene.

I creep away to my room and reflect on what I have just viewed.

Many people come to Plum Village to heal their deep wounds, which may explain the heightened sensitivity and rawness of my fellow pilgrims. When Angelika first arrived at New Hamlet, she hinted that something terrible had happened to her, and that she had come to Plum Village for refuge. She never disclosed the upsetting incident to anyone here. There had been one occasion when the pale-faced German gave the slightest hint that her sadness was due to a romantic heartbreak. It seemed to me that she was making her suffering a hundred times worse by repressing her feelings. In the coming days, post-apocalypse, the shy German would not step back—ever—to allow the toxic argument with the Brazilian to dissipate. Instead she became even more trapped. All of us watched as this meek woman sank deeper into despair—here, at a monastery, of all places. I wondered if Angelika realized that the pain she felt here had nothing to do with the argumentative Brazilian. Perhaps she did. Whenever I looked into Angelika's sad, hollow eyes, I felt utterly helpless. There were all sorts of techniques available to the lost girl, that would have eased her sorrow, yet she appeared to focus solely on the incident with Rita as the roadblock to any possible restoration of her well-being.

Angelika is so completely withdrawn that every time I am near her, I reflect upon my own freedom-busting thoughts and habits.

Habits can absolutely kill us, of course. From my room, I can still hear Rita's passionate pleas and Angelika's cool silence. I think now about the many times I have wanted conditions to be exactly to my liking. When they're not, I have often had the urge to withdraw and run away.

The fallout of that one argument between two pilgrims who each ultimately wanted peace and happiness was that Angelika bolted from the monastery. She packed her bags and fled. The meek, beige-eyed German had planned on staying for a total of four weeks, but in two days she was gone. No one had been able to lift her gloominess. And many tried. But Angelika couldn't accept anyone's gestures—not even from the compassionate nuns. "She's torturing herself," I thought.

During my days here, Thich Nhat Hanh has often talked of this "itch" to escape—thinking that we can somehow avoid the people and things we don't like, and the problems we are experiencing. One day, Thây gave an example of a man who had been so disappointed with his son that he disowned him. The father thought that if he banished his son from the family, all his own troubles would also disappear. Instead, the father lives an agonized life full of regret and sorrow.

Sometime after I returned home from my journey, I read an article in the *Shambhala Sun* by Roshi Joan Halifax, a Buddhist nun who studied for years with Thich Nhat Hanh before founding the Upaya Zen Center with Roshi Bernie Glassman. In the article, Roshi Joan described the Center's core message: *strong back, soft front.* She explained further: "*Strong back* is your capacity to really uphold yourself. *Soft front* is opening to things as they are." Back home, as I pondered this teaching, I recalled this day at New Hamlet, when two wounded women fought so bitterly. The battling Brazilian and German women seemed to have rigid backs rather than strong backs, and rigid fronts rather than soft, fluid fronts. Neither was willing to give an inch, even as they argued in the halls of a Buddhist monastery. I could tell both of them were in a great deal of pain. The softness was there, of course—just buried beneath protective shells and cultural differences. Roshi Joan talks of how compassion comes from nurturing softness toward all life, and upholding that position with strength—especially toward the people you don't particularly like.

Embrace all life around you. Do not run from it.

The delicate, painfully shy, heartbroken, all-beige German bolted from the monastery. I liked Angelika very much and wished I could have found a way to help ease some of her black sadness. At first glance, the hotheaded Brazilian seemed to fare better than the German—she didn't pack her bags and leave—she was facing her demons head-on, not running away. I am sure that resolve will bode well for Rita as she develops her own deep-rooted center of refuge within , even if there are more complications beneath her fiery exterior.

Just before bed tonight, I remember something that Thây said a few days ago. "It is our own selves that make us suffer. We create our own suffering. We are our own worst enemy."

Day 13

Tranquility:
The Nun Who Sang
a French Lullaby

Gently falls asleep the earth
In the evening falling.
Quickly close your eyelids
Sleep my little child.

—FROM AN OLD FRENCH LULLABY

It is late evening and I am lying on the carpeted floor of the meditation hall, in the quiet, candlelit dark, alongside my fellow pilgrims and Sisters of New Hamlet. The candles have shed their golden luster on the insightful phrase that counsels me every morning upon entering the hall: *This is it.* Before closing, my eyes light upon this revelation of Thây's that is gracing the stone wall in a simple frame. One of my favorite nuns (I have many favorites) is gently singing a French song that, from its melody, sounds like a child's lullaby, even though I don't specifically recognize it as one. Sister Prune's voice is ambrosial, and the innocence of the music elicits thoughts of myself as a child with my mother. After three more choral refrains, the boundless music has carried me to another place, a realm of peace where my mother lives.

The singing nun asks me to close my eyes and fall gently into sleep with the earth. More musical refrains cause everything outside of my body to fall away from my senses and I plunge deep within, where I'm embraced by childhood memories. I am a young girl drinking a glass of homemade lemonade in the sun, wearing a blue-flowered, hand-sewn tunic. I become absorbed in the sensation of the memory. The warmth touches me now. I am standing in the courtyard of an Ottawa townhouse with my tanned legs and glints of blond pixie hair, free to own the whole day. I am the girl I was. The buoyancy of the awareness lightens the whole of my body. And then I float on the musical sounds, and the velvet notes themselves transform my memories into astral visions. My mother appears. Her gentle face and graceful strength are with me. Within my body, my mother's quiet, resilient nature awakens.

The moon shines.

I am five years old, lying under the pink and white quilt of my childhood, the orange yarn hair of my favorite soft doll falling beside my sleeping head. My mother has come to my bedside. In the winter night, her warm hand rests softly on my forehead.

Sister Prune sings for me to sleep in peace, beside my mother; to create dreams; and when the morning light comes, I will be joyous.

My mother is here.

Mantras sung with complete devotion produce miracles. When Thây had proclaimed this earlier in the week, I knew it was true. And now I am experiencing the magic.

Every single day, I am reminded that I am one part of the collective whole that is Plum Village. And that Sangha, that community of mindful individuals, together generates a collective energy far more powerful than that of a sole individual. Before every meditation, a nun or monk will call attention to the power of all the people gathered here. The Buddhists of Plum Village call the "gathered" a Sangha body. They remind us that each of us is a cell in the Sangha body, and call for us to chant as one body. Thich Nhat Hanh points out that a group of people established in the Dharma (the teachings of the Buddha) have the power to deal with enormous difficulties in life. Thây has even noted that the teachings of a group do not have to be expressly those of the Buddha. The Sangha group simply must have their minds turned toward compassion and goodness.

I feel the strength of the whole community of New Hamlet now as I vibrate with Sister Prune's transcendent sounds. Not only has she unearthed the healing energy of my mother, but she has also elevated all of us. The wondrous nun has nourished the body of the gathered souls here. She has fed us with her love. And that rapture is palpable. This Buddhist nun has sung with pure devotion and created miracles. My mind has ascended with the mind of each body. My cells have vibrated with the cells of each body. My heart has blossomed with the heart of each body. I am one part of this collective and its exalting power is immense. All of us are cells in the body of the Buddha. And again, I feel fortified on my journey. Diving within, I am taking refuge in my wise self in every moment.

***

The day had been tough. The fiery Brazilian had monopolized what was supposed to be a simple and friendly gathering of the pilgrims of New Hamlet. Rita had used the time to methodically announce a myriad of complaints with regard to the operations of the monastery. First on her list: not enough shelves in her room. "She hasn't been to my room, where there are none," I thought.

Rita's grating monologue went on and on, but early into it, I blocked out much of what she said. Worst of all, the soft-spoken Sister who was monitoring the gathering sat there in perfect silence while the leathery voiced pilgrim rattled off complaints as if the monastery should be run like a five-star hotel. Unlike the gracious nun, I was shocked by the pilgrim's demanding outburst and in awe of the Sister with the patience of Job.

Word to the wise: Do not come to a Buddhist monastery in the damp cold of an Aquitaine winter during a serious meditation retreat and expect luxury. And anyway, extravagance blocks real progress on the spiritual path.

The voice of Sister Prune, having enveloped everybody with magical serenity, gently trails away. I become aware of the room. As my eyes open they again look upon Thây's calligraphy on the wall: *This is it.* I bring myself to my feet. Rita is also standing. She had been lying on the floor, just a few feet from me. Her face is radiant, and appears as smooth as the petal of a lotus. The nun with the miraculous voice has brought the most tranquil of states to all.

The enchantment of the evening plays in my head as I ready myself for bed. How wonderful it would be, I think now, if all of us, aged one to ninety-one, could have children's lullabies sung to us, to dissolve the stress from our adult bodies and invoke images of our loved ones. I will never again think of a lullaby as a song for only a child. And after all, the five-year-old Mary is somewhere inside of me, and she wants to be sung to. It helps soothe the pain.

 Day 14

Stability:
The Man Who Nicked
My Headphones

*He who gains a victory over other men is strong; but he
who gains a victory over himself is all powerful.*

—LAO TZU

Thây's Dharma talks are usually in Vietnamese, so
unless you understand the language, you must use
translation headphones that the monastery provides.
Today inside the Buddha Hall there are several electrical
boxes in between the many blue, square-shaped meditation cushions on the floor. These boxes are used to plug
in the wire extensions from headphones so that one can
hear a translation in English, French, Spanish, Dutch,
or German. The normal procedure is to plug your headphone wires into a box well before the Dharma talk is
set to begin, to secure a spot on the small soundboard.
Sometimes it's difficult to get a working plug, and there
can be sound and equipment problems. Today I do my

usual thing and arrive fifteen minutes early, find a good seat on the English translation side, plug in the wire, and then place the headphones on my cushion. I'm all set up, or so I think.

The morning exercises, a series of ten moving postures called the Ten Mindfulness Exercises created and led by Thây, and the opening chants have finished. The Zen master is about to begin speaking. I put on the headset. There is the normal sound check and everything seems ready to go. My headphones are working fine—I can hear Sister Chan Khong's mellifluous voice. A renowned teacher in her own right, this Sister, whose name points to an essential teaching of the Buddha—True Emptiness—and who will later translate Thây's words from Vietnamese to English, first met Thich Nhat Hanh in 1959 and became ordained by him in 1988. She is a vision of peace. To my right, however, things are far from serene. There is a commotion of whispered activity. I look toward the fraught, hushed sounds and see three anxious-looking people. This group of one man and two women must have arrived late. They are now frantically trying to find free plugs for their own listening devices in the English translation box. I offer to help by signaling to the latecomer closest to me to pass over their three headphone wires. He does just that, and with cables in hand, I attempt to find plugs in the nearby electrical box. But, I can't quite reach, so I temporarily take off my headphones, place them on my cushion, and crawl down the row of seated pilgrims to reach the box. As it turns out, all the plugs are being used, so there is no room for any more wires.

Now, let me just say, I am living in a monastery—I am being taught every day, all day, in every experience, that I should be kind, compassionate, thoughtful, generous, and helpful. "Helpful—yes, I am trying to do that now." And I feel good about it—maybe too good. "At least I tried," I think.

Clutching the wires, I crawl back along the row of cross-legged, understanding pilgrims to my seat as unobtrusively as possible, and put my headphones on. But to my utter bewilderment, there is no sound coming out of them. I am sitting amongst a jumble of wires— it's impossible to see which swirl of coil belongs where. Perplexed, I attempt to decipher the masses of entwined cables that surround my legs. "What's wrong?" I wonder. "My headphones were working, I had been so careful to plug them into a working electrical box."

The room goes quiet. Thây is now speaking. I am missing the words of a Buddhist scholar. Another five soundless minutes go by and I almost resign myself to listening to the talk in Vietnamese. Then something occurs to me. "I wonder if one of the latecomers took my headphones—could that be?" I think this because the man whom I had attempted to assist is now cheerfully sitting with a listening device on his head, happy as a clam, obviously hearing English words. "Excuse me," I say to him. "Did you take my headphones?" The clam stares at me blankly, his smile diminishing. Guilty. I ask him the same question again, this time firmly. He casually responds that he does, in fact, have my headphones. I instantly fume. "Um, please give them back to me." As I say this, my fellow pilgrim, absent of embarrassment, casually removes the device from his head, as if nothing out of the ordinary has happened.

There is something about finding yourself in a Buddhist place of worship with a head that is about to explode.

While I was crawling over the folded legs of my quiet neighbors in an attempt to find working plugs for this man and his two friends, and while a wise monk was talking about wise things, this man replaced my headphones with his—the unplugged ones with no sound. Yes, that's what he did. Did I already mention that every day here, we are being taught to be kind?

For the next five minutes I sit here seething. I do not hear a word that Thây says, even though I now have English sounds coming into my ears. Instead, my wild thoughts go something like this: "How could that man do such a thing to me? I was the one trying to help him when no one else would. And then he goes and takes *my* headphones? What a betrayal. What a selfish man! And here, of all places, at a Buddhist monastery." Multiple variations of this diatribe dominate the space in my mind.

Then a few words that Thây says trickle into my hot head: "Go to your 'in' breath. Go to your 'out' breath. Then your consciousness will be pushed inside of you, where you feel safe. Your breath nourishes you, heals you. Take good care of the island of your self—it is beautiful in there." And I finally start to pay attention to this master teacher.

"Go to your breath."

My eyes close. My breath moves in 1, 2, 3, 4, pause. My breath moves out 1, 2, 3, 4, pause. I do this again, and again, and again. My awareness buoys my breath and is a beacon for my renewal. The nourishing air flows in, and it flows out—even, continuous, rhythmic, and deep. My concentrated breath guides me to a secure place inside. And the revolution begins.

"Create sunshine for yourself. Do not go outside for beauty and sunshine. Then, when there is a storm outside, you will know how to go back to your self. Put peace inside of you."

Boulders of tension roll off my shoulders, stiffness melts from my spine, furrows on my brow become smooth as silk, and layers of anguish peel away. I am breathing with my breath.

"Bring your safe island with you wherever you go."

My resentment breaks down. Anger disappears. I am light.

"In the stormy ocean of life, take refuge in your self."

I have taken refuge.

It is ten o'clock in the evening; I have brushed my teeth, and am now lying on my cot. I pick up the *Tao Te Ching*, a book of sacred and ancient teachings that I had brought with me from Canada. This manual, *the way of life*, is a compilation of wisdom from the Chinese master Lao Tzu from around the sixth century BC. I close my eyes, hold the book in my hands, and randomly open it to a page. One line from the stanza leaps out.

"If you blame others, there will be no end to your blame."

There's nothing like having your comfortable thoughts challenged.

Since returning home from the monastery, when I have felt wronged in some way, I remember this incident with headphone man. And then a liberating feeling comes over me. What if I am able to let go of everything in my life? That even includes those times when I have been really crossed. Like the time I had my brand new iPhone stolen at a restaurant, along with my favorite chestnut brown leather purse, wallet, ID, and house keys. What if I don't blame the thief? It's not always possible to predict if an event will lead to good fortune or bad fortune.

Stephen Mitchell, a modern translator of the *Tao Te Ching*, recounts an ancient tale that highlights our inability to predict outcomes accurately. The story is of a farmer whose prized horse bolts away. The farmer's neighbors extend their sympathies toward the farmer for his loss. The farmer responds by asking: "How do I know if this is bad fortune or good fortune?" The horse eventually comes back to the farm, having bred with another horse of even higher stock, making the farmer very wealthy. The farmer's neighbors again come calling, this time to congratulate him. Yet the farmer only asks: "How do I know if this is good fortune or bad fortune?" While riding the horse, the farmer's eighteen-year-old son falls off and breaks his leg. The neighbors come round to express their sorrow in the farmer's bad luck, especially since the injured son will no longer be able to help tend the farm. The farmer again remains composed. Soon after, war breaks out in the country and all the young men are conscripted to military service. Ninety percent of the men die in the battle. Of course, the farmer's son, with his broken leg, is saved from going to war.

Having my iPhone stolen that bleak night in a Toronto restaurant woke me up to reality and strengthened my discipline. The incident reminded me that life is not a dream, and that I must keep my eyes wide open and my mind sharply focused. That night I also had a painful reminder of the truth that actions matter. I must watch my *own* actions. Because of that robbery, I went on to clean up an area of my life that needed attention. The painful incident caused me to become intensely aware of my own responsibility toward honesty.

In *The Heart of the Buddha's Teachings*, Thây recognizes that "Obstacles teach us about our strengths and weaknesses, so that we can know ourselves better and see in which direction we truly wish to go."

Experiencing thievery, in a Buddhist place of worship no less, was an obstacle that challenged me to dive deeper into the calming and nourishing power of my breath, even while the whole thing reeked of sacrilege. Come to think of it, having an iPhone is a kind of religious experience, and the theft of one can feel sinfully irreverent. Victory over the self, however, no matter what storm is happening outside—now that's a power that reigns supreme.

⇝ Day 15 ⇜

Clarity:
An "Enemy" Helps Me See the
Truth of Inter-Being

*I am he, as you are he, as you are me, and we are all
together.*

—THE BEATLES

I am in the meditation hall translating an American pilgrim's thoughts into French for a Sister who does not
understand English. It's all going along swimmingly when
suddenly, and in a strikingly nasty way, Vanna accuses me
of misrepresenting her in my translation. God knows how
she would think that, as she doesn't understand a word of
French. At first I'm stunned into silence, and then anger
fills that dead hole. It's as if I was just waiting for a good
excuse to despise my fellow pilgrim.

Sometimes you meet people that you simply do not
like. These people don't even have to utter a word, and
yet somehow their very presence annoys you. Living at

a monastery does not change this reality. Not everyone gets along.

I met Vanna during the drive to the monastery, on my arrival day. She was aloof—she might have glanced at me and the other woman in the van once, but never said a word during the entire forty-minute journey to Plum Village, and not even to the amiable nun driving the van. Of course one never knows why someone acts a particular way, and one should always foster compassion toward others but, you know, sometimes there are people . . .

Vanna regularly has loud crying fits in her room from which no one is able to calm her. The wails appear to be a little fake, and mostly attention-seeking. But that's only my opinion and I'm probably wrong—I know I'm wrong. However, there is one thing that is just downright dense. On cold mornings, Vanna wears a huge winter coat in the meditation hall, and every time she moves, the gigantic parka makes an irritating rustling sound, which I find terribly distracting while meditating. I feel alone with this annoyance, however, because no one ever says a word to her about it. And, yes, such minor issues become weirdly important when one is living in close quarters for many days with lots of people.

There's more. During group discussions surrounding Thây's teachings of the day, Vanna often launches into long-winded and tedious monologues, which center on her own life rather than the suggested topic of examination. I find myself actively trying to avoid the groups that Vanna joins. A head-on crash between us was only a matter of time. In the real world I may be able to steer clear of the people I don't like. Not here— it's impossible. I have to live with Vanna. I have to meditate, eat, walk, and sit in discussion with a person who grates on my nerves.

Now, since the translation debacle, I can't even stand the sight of Vanna. I think of the masterful Thich Nhat Hanh's words: "When you look deeply at what is out there, you see yourself." And then not only do I revile the innocent pilgrim, but I feel confusion and dismay, too. "There is no way I am remotely like that selfish and aloof woman," I think.

I often hear the Sisters talk of "watering the positive seeds" in people, which simply means acting and speaking in a way that encourages a person's best qualities and feelings to blossom. Buddhists talk of there being many layers to our consciousness. One of those layers, store consciousness, is described by Thich Nhat Hanh as the part of our consciousness that receives and processes information and then preserves that data in what are called "seeds," or *bijas*. All of us have positive seeds such as mindfulness, joy, love, and compassion within us, along with negative ones such as discrimination, anger, hate, and greed. Sometimes circumstances, other people, or even our history of ancestral conditioning touch these negative seeds within us and cause them to sprout into our mind consciousness—this top layer where we actively think and experience these sprouted seeds as mental formations or energies. Once manifested up in the mind consciousness, these energies flourish and we feel them.

Somehow, I water Vanna's negative seed of anger. And there is something about Vanna's way of being that touches that same destructive emotion within me.

Earlier in the week, Thây had drawn a circle on the blackboard with a vertical line through the middle to represent the mind and its simultaneous containment of *subject* and *object*. "They are born at the same time and exist together. The perceiver and perceived manifest at the same time."

Upon returning home from my journey, I would recall this teaching while looking at the vibrant jade plant in my kitchen. Every time I looked at it, the plant *seemed* like an object that existed outside of my conscious viewing of it—until I focused more deeply. Thây tells me that if I think that any object exists outside of my consciousness, I am making a very basic error. I would be falling prey to double grasping, a problematic way of thinking that contains two wrong views. One mistake is in thinking that the mind is separate; the second error comes from thinking that the object of the mind is separate. If I think, for example, that the jade plant is something outside of myself that has nothing to do with me, as a conscious being viewing it, then I would be wrong. "Consciousness is always consciousness of something," Thây said.

It is far more pleasant for me to consider the subject/object link with something I enjoy—like my living green jade plant—rather than a person I am not very fond of.

"God and me are one. If you are able to look very deeply, you will see that you and God are not separate."

Yes, a Buddhist monk uttered this phrase. Earlier in the week during one of his talks, Thây explained this union of subjects and objects, "Usually people have the view that there is a *creator* and a *creature*. But the truth is that the *creature* contains the *creator*, the *daughter* contains the *mother*. We think that the mother is born before the daughter." At first, I thought Thây was simply teaching us to change our construct of time as linear, which I was quite comfortable with. But then he said this beautiful thing: "A mother only becomes a mother when her child is born." And that of course makes all the sense in the world and is quite true. Looked at this way, the mother and child are quite clearly born together. I now simply need to apply this way of thinking to all subjects and objects.

Thây wrote this on the blackboard:

(1) TRANSMITTER = (2) OBJECT OF TRANSMISSION = (3) RECEIVER = EMPTINESS OF TRANSMISSION.

This is called the three phases of transmission. A subject and object *inter-are*—they co-exist. The first helps bring the second to life, but they manifest simultaneously—they lean on each other in order to exist. They are also empty of a separate, independent self.

So if I am not able to be civilized toward Vanna, the French translation-bashing American, then I am unable to truly value myself. If I think that I— the subject—am *truly* separate from Vanna, the object of my viewing, and the person with whom I am having an experience, then I am mistaken. Her way of being is dependent on mine—we lean on each other. This goes much deeper than the reality that we have unique appearances in the world. If I think that we exist independently of each other, and are not made up of the same elements of the world, then I am dead wrong. I am actively discriminating against a fellow human being. I am not accepting the truth that I co-exist with Vanna. I am caught in my one view and that perspective is erroneous and narrow.

The truth is, my fellow human being and I are made up of exactly the same universal elements. And we are manifesting simultaneously. Both of us are empty of a separate self but full of the whole universe. Emptiness is a most valuable tool that Buddhists use to delve more deeply into the true nature of things. If I can understand that the whole cosmos has come together to create Vanna, me, you, my vibrant green jade plant, the pale brown wrens of this French countryside, and everything else here on earth, then I am in touch with the teachings of the Buddha. If I can take care of my negative seed of anger by encouraging my positive seed of mindfulness to recognize, and then embrace that destructive mental formation, then that anger will weaken. Fighting or suppressing that energy once it has manifested will do me no good. Mindfulness has the power to propel me up above the negativity. And with practice, perhaps those negative seeds will arise less often. Thây calls this being "skillful" with our emotions: "You do not have to die because of one emotion." Maybe I could even find ways to water the positive seeds within Vanna instead of the negative ones. That would be a great thing.

Like Buddhist insights, yogic teachings counsel recognizing that the *other person* is *you*.

Thây has regularly emphasized that developing clarity of mind and embodying the truth that all of us are very deeply interconnected is essential for our happiness and well-being. When we are confused, we suffer very deeply. A clear mind is essential for developing a sterling sanctuary within. Every one of us benefits from a mind that is as clear and pristine as a blue lotus pool.

I remember reading NASA scientist John Oro's forecast: "When people look at earth from outside, something strange and revolutionary will happen: people will alter their thinking." I think of the photos of the earth revealing the planet's magnificent swirls of blue taken from the moon. This globe that we're on in this vast, black universe. We're all floating together in space on one tiny planet. We're all interdependent and interconnected. We should trust the astronaut's view. The Beatles also got it right.

≈ Day 16 ≈

Faith:
Beginning Anew

Faith is the ability to not panic.

—ANONYMOUS

The evening meditations have just finished. Three silent Sisters, eyes lowered, walk halfway up the center aisle of the meditation hall, pause, bring their hands into a prayerful posture, and then bow their heads, first toward the radiant Buddha statue and then to the Sisters and pilgrims gathered here. One of the three begins to speak: "We are so very thankful and fortunate to live here in Plum Village with the love and support of the Buddha, Dharma, and Sangha." With her proclamation, this Sister is taking refuge in The Three Jewels, a fundamental practice in Buddhism that helps one to feel safe and secure. She recognizes that the Buddha shows her the way in life, and this *way* or Dharma is the path of understanding, compassion, and love. The Sangha she talks of is the community of Sisters that she lives with in harmony and awareness. The Sister continues speaking:

"We would like to say how deeply sorry we are for our momentary lack of mindfulness yesterday, which caused problems within our community. We vow to renew our mindfulness."

The spokesperson for the three nuns is simply following a regular ritual at Plum Village called "Beginning Anew," a practice of reconciliation that can happen between two people or as a group. There are four steps to the practice: sharing appreciation, sharing regret, expressing hurt, and sharing difficulties. The idea is that through the verbal expression of regretful actions, done unknowingly or knowingly, against a person or the community, further misunderstandings can be avoided and then awareness and appreciation for that person or community can be cultivated.

This contrite Sister made a special request to practice Beginning Anew this evening, but these ceremonies, with the whole community of New Hamlet, happen regularly. So far, during my stay, there have been two of these therapeutic sessions in which all of the Sisters and pilgrims had gathered in one of the halls, sat quietly in a circle, and then, one by one, confessed.

About a week ago, during my first experience with this healing ceremony, I had quietly watched as various Sisters and pilgrims each picked up a small vase of yellow tulips, placed it before their confessional knees, and then announced some past regret. One older Sister had spoken of her deep love for her community of Sisters: She had recognized how diligently all of them worked and expressed her regret for not being physically robust enough to help keep up the monastery. She'd had difficulty accepting that reality.

The communal aspect of this confessional sharing looked to be way more fun than my Catholic school confessions had ever been, in those small, enclosed booths, with some faceless priest hidden on one side of a dark screen. Upon hearing a few more of these Buddhist-style confessions, I recalled that, a few days ago, I had carelessly forgotten about my working meditation of raking leaves. I thought that now might be a good time to fess up. So, at the next pause, following the ritual as everyone else had, I went into the circle, picked up the vase of tulips, and said, "I am thankful for the great kindness and generosity of all the Sisters." In the next moment, as soon as I said, "the Sister's arms open wide to all of the many visitors," I shamelessly began bawling—the kind of crying that becomes a heaving, because of a simultaneous attempt to speak.

The sensation of relief in declaring my transgression, though minor, was immediate. And this may have been the reason for my tears. But mostly, the ritual had provided a valuable structure to my thoughts. Offering my thanks aloud, I had realized the generous nature of the Sisters of New Hamlet. If those thoughts had remained in my head, and had never been properly uttered, their greater meaning might have been lost to me. On that evening, for the first time during my pilgrimage, I had identified the power of the Sangha. From that day on, I became aware of the source behind my feelings of elevation. Essentially, the group was serving as a forklift for my spirit. The community of Plum Village was supporting my journey to build an unwavering, abiding power within. Keeping company with those turned toward liveliness of spirit and truth was clearing the pain of losing my loving parents and boosting my resolve to understand how to better navigate the turbulent waters of life. Recognizing that I was one part of this greater whole, one cell of the Buddha body, was easing my feelings of loneliness, because the energy of this community is so high.

Remembering the truth that, at times, every one of us experiences difficulties, eases personal suffering. The band R.E.M. got it right when they sang: "Everybody hurts sometimes."

It is imperative that we surround ourselves with people who truly care for us. Some people in our lives do not support us. Thich Nhat Hanh emphasizes that we must spend our valuable time with compassionate, caring, and loving people. Otherwise we won't be happy. I believe him.

Some days the magnifying power of the Sangha feels immense, as when Sister Prune sang that beautiful lullaby a few days ago. On other days, the dynamism is surely there, but with a lighter weight to it, like a soft blanket over a grateful body.

The fruits of the individual and collective action are interconnected.

All our actions are connected, and of an interdependent nature. Thây often mentions the *collective karma* or actions of those living at the monastery. The collective is simply made up of all the individuals together, and therefore it is important to recognize that the actions of the individual within the collective certainly impact that collective.

In many of the Buddha's sutras, there are tales of the Buddha conversing with "those that doubted." After all, the Buddha was only one of several spiritual teachers in India at the time. But, importantly, the Buddha did not try to convince anyone that his method of liberation was the only true path. In his book, *Joyful Wisdom*, Yongey Mingyur Rinpoche summarizes what the Buddha's view would have been in modern terms: "This is just what I did, and this is what I recognized. Don't believe anything I say because I say so. Try it out for yourselves."

Like Yongey Mingyur, Thich Nhat Hanh advises us to test out the efficacy of the Buddha's teachings for ourselves. He advises us to look for evidence that our meditation and studies are creating positive change within us, and to not take any teaching on blind faith. It is necessary to personally investigate the teachings. That makes a lot of sense to me.

The word *faith* has become associated with a definition: belief that is not based on proof. Another meaning is simply the following: confidence or trust in a person or thing. This doesn't imply that we haven't investigated that person or thing in order to have that faith. During my pilgrimage, I regularly investigate faith.

Earlier today, as I picked some romaine lettuce leaves in the garden, I realized that those leaves, of course, came from romaine lettuce seeds. Potatoes will not come from the seeds of romaine lettuce. But if someone told me that potatoes grow from romaine lettuce seeds, would I blindly believe them? No. Thây has taught me to observe and investigate, for myself, the genesis of everything. It is the same thing with spiritual teachings. On the wise advice of a Zen master, I am investigating for myself what is being presented here and seeing if it works.

All the Sisters in the meditation hall tonight are displaying faith. They trust that a monastic life, immersed in the teachings of the Buddha, is a path of awakening. The faith these nuns have in the spiritual practices, this Beginning Anew ceremony tonight, and all the various rituals of Plum Village, display trust rather than blind acceptance. With their daily work, the Sisters of New Hamlet actively experiment—they test out these particular teachings, and thus see for themselves if the counsel of the Buddha works. That, to me, is the definition of faith.

Everyone has now left the meditation hall, after the final bow that signaled the completion of the Beginning Anew ceremony. The contrite and gentle Sister who had been speaking is one of the nuns I regularly enjoy spending time with, so after the hall empties I walk over to her. I am curious about the reason for her mea culpa. Often, people will indicate specifics during these ceremonies, but tonight, this Sister did not. I ask her what happened yesterday—what caused her such regret. It turns out that while the three nuns had been driving to the village, one of them hadn't had a seatbelt on, and the French police had noticed and stopped the car. Two of the Sisters in the car were of Vietnamese origin, and the police had asked about their immigration papers, which one Sister did not have. This led to complications for the whole Plum Village community.

Everything is interconnected.

It's wonderful to be reminded that blind faith is unwise. And to ensure that this lazy quality doesn't sneak into my mind. I am enjoying this investigating. It gives me faith, and faith makes me feel strong—like I am Home.

~ Day 17 ~

Kindness:
The Woman Who Made Me Soup

When I was young, I used to admire intelligent people; as I grow older, I admire kind people.
— ABRAHAM JOSHUA HESCHEL

"Bonjour, mademoiselle, ça va?" I am lingering at the farmers' market in a small village nearby the monastery, gazing at purple beets, when a local French woman asks me how I am doing.

"Oui, merci, ça va," I am fine, I answer. And thus begins my lovely day, with a lovely woman, in a lovely village. Brigette puts two dark green zucchinis into her shopping bag and promises to pay the farmer next time— the wonder of small villages, you can take now and pay later. The next thing I know, I have been adopted like a lost and hungry cat.

Brigette insists on making me lunch at her home. Without waiting for my reply, the amiable villager walks me to her silver blue Citroen, then opens the car door and apologizes for the *Babar the Elephant* book on the front seat. We're now in the car and on our way to Brigette's country home, perched on one of the many nearby hills. When we arrive, I am invited in to a quaint cottage-like bungalow and asked to sit down at the kitchen table. Brigette begins washing and chopping a zucchini. Before long the Frenchwoman has whipped up a delicious-looking soup and plunked a steaming bowl in front of me. Through spoons of dark green puree and mouthfuls of crusty bread—those baked masterpieces of the French—the two of us chat about Buddhist practices and Plum Village. When I happen to mention my relentlessly sore shoulders, Brigette promptly offers to give me a therapeutic massage, as she is a trained therapist. Before I know it, I am having one of those rare moments of feeling absolutely alien to myself. I am naked on a table (okay, a thin sheet covers me) in a remote French cottage, and on my bare back are the hands of a woman I have known for exactly one hour. The massage is technically not that great, and Brigette keeps chattering in quick French the whole time I am trying to relax, but that is absolutely beside the point. This exceptionally genial stranger has paid loving attention to me, and that, in and of itself, zaps the iciness from my shoulders. After the treatment, Brigette insists on driving me back to the monastery, a one-and-a-half-hour journey by foot. And she lends me her extra-warm sweater after I mention that, stupidly, I didn't bring enough proper clothes with me from Canada.

"Right," I think. "How many times have I invited a stranger into my home, prepared soup for her, put clothes on her back, and ferried her around by car? Oh, and obliterated the tension in her shoulders to boot? Ummm, let me think . . . Never."

"Let no one ever come to you without leaving better and happier. Be the living expression of God's kindness: kindness in your face, kindness in your eyes, kindness in your smile."

Brigette has taken a page from Mother Teresa here. She doesn't know it, but the woman who made me soup has stood in for my absent mother. Thank God for surrogate mothers.

I see a great deal of benevolence and generosity of spirit living with the nuns of Plum Village. The Sisters put the visitors before themselves. And it's not like they have it easy. It is challenging work to keep a gigantic monastery spread across four Hamlets running smoothly, and yet many of the nuns smile and gesture for others to go ahead of them in the food line, for example. When one Sister had a severe cold for a period of time, I saw her continue to rise at dawn and keep up her demanding work around the residence without a single complaint. Perhaps the strength of their Sisterhood is the reason for the nun's skill. Thây has more than once emphasized the importance of being in a loving, caring environment—of placing yourself amongst kind and supportive people in order to thrive. This is really starting to sink in. Those who truly support you with the fullness of their being are precious jewels. These gems are happy for your happiness, and their authenticity will keep you strong both mentally and physically.

Brigette drops me at the front steps of New Hamlet, her thick knit sweater warming my shoulders as I bid her a French goodbye. I walk through the door and into the dining hall to see my friend Hannah, a lovely Dutch woman, courteous almost to a fault. Hannah has lent Rita, the hot-tempered Brazilian, her thermos for tea because Rita has been complaining daily about an illness that never seems to arrive. Rita has had Hannah's thermos for over a week now, and Rita is still not sick. But now Hannah *is* sick. Hannah needs her thermos back so she can have hot ginger tea for her sore throat close at hand. Here's what happens at the tea stand before dinner—Rita sees that Hannah has a cold, but doesn't offer to return Hannah's thermos. I mention to Rita that the ill Dutchwoman should have her thermos back. The Brazilian stares blankly. Rita can't quite seem to loosen her grip on Hannah's thermos, but she does say that she will try to arrange for someone to buy another thermos when they go into town. This won't be easy. We are in the middle of the winter monastic retreat, and the nuns need special permission to go shopping—and then only for necessities. After asking several Sisters, Rita can't manage to find anyone available to go into town for a new thermos, so she just keeps Hannah's thermos. There it is—Rita is not sick. Hannah is. Rita does not return the tea thermos that is Hannah's to start with. Hannah is far more gracious than I ever would have been under the same circumstances. I have the odd feeling of being one of a group of juvenile girls, quibbling at summer camp.

A gong rings, three adolescent girls scatter, and dissatisfaction hangs in the air. The silence in the dinner line only serves to highlight the discontent within these monastery walls this evening. I look around the room. The nun with the beautiful face is standing by the fireplace looking tired and sad; an older Sister who looks to be in physical discomfort is wincing and shifting her weight from foot to foot; the pale and sick Hannah is standing with no tea flask; and a myriad of equally distressed souls are milling about. All of us are immersed in our own thoughts, but those musings are sometimes easily read on transparent faces. I look over toward a fellow pilgrim. She is the sole person smiling, and she is grinning like a child. I realize that she is excited about the meal tonight. It must be something she enjoys, because on other days I have seen her scowl in the dinner line. I watch the pilgrim become extremely excited—I mean overjoyed—looking at the yummy dinner. This same woman bolted from another Hamlet to get away from a roommate there. "Our happiness is often so directly related to our circumstances," I think. When things are to our liking, of course, we are very happy. But if events do not unfold as we wish, what then? I remember something Thây said: "You must realize that you already have enough conditions in your life to be happy."

⚜

Shortly after returning home from my pilgrimage, I read Bill Clinton's *Giving*. In the book, Clinton talks of models of generosity coming from different people who had never had an opportunity to make much money, and could only afford the very basics needed to live.

One of those people is Oseola McCarty. She gave $150,000 of her hard-earned money, saved from washing and ironing clothes for seventy-five years, to the University of Southern Mississippi to endow a scholarship fund for African-American students. As I read the book and reflected on Ms. McCarty, I thought, "I bet she *really* washed those clothes and that is why she is wise."

There is an ancient tale about a famous Zen Buddhist master that displays the power unleashed when deeply immersed in a task. This particular teacher had been responsible for erecting one hundred sacred temples in the East, a difficult and important task. A student asked him, "Master, you must have gained immeasurable merit for the building of these beautiful temples where so many people meditate and pray." The teacher responded, "The merit from building one hundred temples is nothing compared to the merit I will gain if I wash this one dish properly."

Oseola McCarty *knew* how to wash clothes.

The nuns of New Hamlet follow a Buddhist practice called *Dana Paramita*. The Sisters have told me that this wise teaching expands their capacity for being generous under all conditions. If, for example, a Sister is angry with a fellow nun, she will send a gift to her. When I first heard of this unique method of gift giving, I tried to imagine doing it. I couldn't imagine it. But the Buddha said that if you can find it in your heart to make this kind gesture, immediately your anger will dissipate— and not only that, you will likely receive a lovely and positive response from the beneficiary of your elevated gesture. This is a noble idea, but sometimes in the tough real world it's not possible to make a dent in those with very hardened shells. Back home in Toronto, after upsetting a man I had been dating briefly, I sent him a long-stemmed orange gerber daisy to apologize. Not only did I never hear from him again, but the toughened soul didn't acknowledge the gesture at all. And come on—how often does a woman send a man a flower? The Buddha is right, though—even a very small benevolent act invokes warm feelings no matter what the response.

The Buddha knew that one's own suffering is relieved through helping others.

My surrogate French mother, Brigette, seemed to be quite a happy person, even though she told me that she has had a challenging life. A single mother, strapped for cash, with no family close by, there were many reasons for her to be a grump, but she wasn't one. She was only kind and generous. I ponder the truth that all of us inherently *know*—kind acts foster happiness within the practitioner of that generosity.

I resolve to be more kind.

⤳ Day 18 ⤶

Humility, Part Two: Losing a PhD

Be compassionate, for everyone you meet is fighting a great battle.

—IAN MACLAREN

Rita is the kind of person one feels slightly uncomfortable around. It comes from a worry that she might suddenly bite your head off, as she did with Angelika, the wounded German. I've noticed that people tend to keep their distance from the hotheaded Brazilian.

It's lunchtime, and Rita is sitting at one of the dining tables all alone. A bit reluctantly, I walk over and sit down with her. She looks happy to see me. It's not long before Rita tells me about her many years of work on a dissertation for her PhD. Rita says that, at one point, the evaluation committee requested that she change some of the content in the dissertation. As we sit here, cradling cups of green tea, Rita continues on with her story: "The committee didn't understand my work, so I decided not to make the adjustments." I can guess what's coming next. "I submitted my work to the committee anyway, without the changes, and they decided not to give me my PhD," she exclaimed. "Can you believe it?" Yes, I thought, I can believe that they did not give you a PhD. But I do not say this aloud.

All actions cause repercussions of some sort. In Buddhist teachings, there are two kinds of karma. The first kind comes back very quickly, and is sometimes referred to as "instant karma." For example, if I punch you in the face, you may punch me right back, and I will have instantly experienced the fruit of my action.

The second kind of karma comes back some time later. I worry more about this type of karma. In his book *Buddha Mind, Buddha Body*, Thich Nhat Hanh uses the example of writing a bad check to shed light on how this karma plays out. If you were to write a check with not enough money in your bank account, you wouldn't feel any repercussions for maybe a week, but you can be sure that eventually you would suffer negative consequences from signing that bad check.

We could hazard a pretty good guess as to what the particular outcome would be from bouncing a check. But we can't be one hundred percent sure. I try to remember that it is next to impossible to predict the many possible outcomes that could come from any of the things I have thought, said, or done. And that uncertainty is dangerous. One could potentially unknowingly jeopardize many years of diligent, hard work on a PhD, for example. There is also the possibility of a seemingly benign action, if left alone, building in strength and causing an effect far surpassing its original weight.

I once heard a yogi describe karma like this:

> You think you have simply kicked a pebble
> at the top of a mountain, but that small
> stone could gather moss and dirt and rub-
> bish as it tumbles downhill, and that stone

could become very large, and then it could very possibly and devastatingly crash into some person or thing at the bottom of that mountain.

The only condition that first action needed was time. For you to accurately predict what is at the base, and how long that pebble will take to roll down the mountain, is virtually impossible.

All causes are also effects and all effects are also causes. There are multiple causes for one effect; multiple effects come from just one cause. Again, presuming to know the exact outcome from any action is not possible. This is why mindfulness is your best friend.

"The energy of mindfulness contains concentration and insight. The energy of concentration contains mindfulness and insight. The energy of insight contains mindfulness and concentration."

There is great power in these three sentences of Thich Nhat Hanh's. Taking a bit of time to be mindful could very well save you from engaging in some very unfortunate behavior.

The auburn-haired Brazilian has gone to refill her teacup, and I sit here alone pondering Thây's interconnected insights. Just outside the window in front of me, I see forests of tall bamboo plants in the garden. My focus hones in on these beauties. The sacred stalks must have come from very far away, perhaps Japan. They are old and ancient, even as they are fresh and alive. The smooth, pale green shafts come in varying heights, and their sage color is luminescent. The plants are motionless until a gentle breeze reveals their pliancy. I imagine their intertwined roots deep in the earth—those life-giving vessels, hidden away from my eyes. Water fills those roots and is sucked up, way up through the body of the plant. The bamboo plant is there—quiet, resolute, full of history and energy.

My lonely friend has come back with a fresh cup of hot, green tea. I am pulled away from the forest of bamboo. It is not comfortable to sit here right now. I would rather be back with the bamboo plants. A thick, negative air hangs about Rita—a real gloominess, even though I can tell she simply wants to be happy like all of us. Before long, the pilgrim's despair has seeped into my skin until I feel quite depressed.

For the next few moments, I tune Rita out. I look through the window and notice one bamboo plant, in the center of the forest, its contented height resting in the middle of the surrounding stalks. "Be moderate, like this resolute bamboo plant," I counsel myself. Charging ahead full force, armed with blind ambition, will only end in a big disappointing and perhaps deadly crash. Gazing at the bamboo, I recall the time I had boldly run in front of a bus, thinking I could safely cross the street, only to be very nearly run over by a speeding car passing the bus. I'm pretty sure I gave that driver a heart attack. Careless mistakes can be fatal. Prudent humility is a steady power. And with that insight I feel more awake and connected to the wise place of refuge within. Intelligent humility is beautiful. Blind self confidence is not. And again, it all comes back to the Buddha's enlightened insight—walk the middle path.

Authenticity:
How *Not* To Be Sneaky

Decency is the absence of strategy.

—CHOGYAM TRUNGPA

At exactly noon today, a childish comedy begins. I am standing on the grass outside the main building of New Hamlet when a few shaven heads in brown robes come into my view, ambling along the road. I catch my breath. A fellow pilgrim is crouching behind a small gate, whispering curses. Helena should be with the other pilgrims at the lay-friend's gathering.

Today the monastics have gone to Thây's hermitage, the location of which remains secret to all but the Brothers and Sisters of Plum Village—which only serves to enhance the intrigue of the day. Today, in this mysterious abode, the monks and nuns will receive special, monastic-only teachings while the pilgrims will gather at Lower Hamlet, a second residence for nuns, to partake in the once-weekly lay-friend's gathering. I don't like these days. They are structured like this: a circle "meet and greet;" a choice of several activities throughout the day that may include singing, sharing lunch, discussing Thây's teachings, and yoga sessions. This last thing may be the reason for my aversion. One time a fellow pilgrim led a "laughing yoga" session, and the forced jolliness almost made me cry. Don't *ask* me to laugh, just *make* me laugh. A few senior students are in charge of these organized events, most of which would be fine, enjoyable even, like last week's creative writing workshop organized by the cat-killing Newfoundlander, but they can also feel a bit odd, like playtime for adults. I prefer all the monks and nuns and pilgrims together. In my mind, the presence of the monastics elevates the atmosphere. To be honest, I'm kind of a monastic snob. My exaltation of the ascetics only heightened when I learned about their hidden headquarters of enigmatic Buddhist teachings. I do not like seeing this side of myself. I would rather be a joyful participant in any activity. And of course, I do end up gaining valuable insights from everyone here—in all situations.

Because of my disaffection for these gatherings, I had submitted a request to the head Sister, the Abbot of New Hamlet, to stay at the residence, away from the lay-friends' day. I claimed that I had writing to catch up on. The abbot had generously granted my request. Only here's what happened next. When I mentioned I was staying back to my neighbor Helena, she thought that would be a good idea for her as well. She didn't have a good excuse, though. So my partner in hidden crime decided to feign illness.

The nuns soon came around, calling for us to get in the van to travel to the neighboring Hamlet, where all the lay-friends were to meet. From my room, I heard a Sister knock on Helena's door. Silence. Then there was a bit of a commotion—I think they saw right through her façade. While this was happening, I was sitting on the floor of my own room, scribbling notes in my journal while pangs of guilt jabbed at me. It's uncomfortable being a witness to the deception of a virtuous nun—and I knew that Helena got the idea to play hooky from me. But I also felt foolishly justified. *I* was granted permission, and from the abbot, no less. I certainly hadn't revealed my real reason for wanting to stay back—that I disliked these scheduled days. Of course the abbot wouldn't have granted my request if she'd known that.

The Tibetan Buddhist Chogyam Trungpa would have had something to say about my little scheme . . .

> Decency means that you are not cheating anybody at all. You are not even about to cheat anybody. There is a sense of straight-forwardness and simplicity . . . Decency is the absence of strategy. It is of utmost importance to realize that [one's] approach should be . . . simple and straightforward. That makes it very beautiful: you have nothing up your sleeve; therefore, a sense of genuineness comes through. That is decency.

I wonder why these wandering monks are not yet at the hermitage? Helena continues to hide behind the gate, while I stand out front to signal when the coast is clear. I smile toward the gentle face of the innocent monk passing by, and my annoyance with Helena escalates. I feel drawn into this game of deception that I had no interest in.

Did I say the day is a disaster? And by the way, the muck really stinks down here.

Just as the ambling monks pass out of sight, three more brown-robed visions appear. Embarrassed, I cast my eyes down from the grey clouds and into the grassy ground, where I notice a dead field mouse. Its dark blood is still fresh on the brown of its neck, and its tail is in a perfect limp spiral around a tuft of grass. The corpse is even more intimidating because one black eye is open and the other is hanging from a torn shred of tendon, or some such thing. I wonder if the rodent was attacked by a wandering cat, or the neighboring farmer's big, black dog—the canine that had ominously followed me one day, during a long walk up in the hills amongst the apple tree plantation, with not another human soul in sight. The menacing beast had shadowed me as I imagined the newspaper report: "Canadian woman viciously attacked by rabid dog in remote French countryside, dies of wounds in hospital."

The last of the monks have finally disappeared just as the taxi pulls up in front of New Hamlet. The previously concealed pilgrim and I climb in the yellow car, finally off to the village for lunch. Stress, however, comes along for the ride. Dishonesty takes a toll on one's whole being. It is much healthier to be straightforward. Sneakiness is exhausting. The taxi drops us off in front of the restaurant and we walk in to a dining room full of French villagers drinking red wine at noon. Both of us order mushroom omelets and *frites* from the unassuming waitress who shows surprise when we refuse glasses of Bordeaux. Before long, I am putting forkfuls of carefully prepared eggs into my mouth, but I am not eating a delicious mushroom omelet. Instead, I am eating despair, as Thich Nhat Hanh would say. And it tastes sour.

I imagine my judicious fellow pilgrims are happily noshing on nutty brown rice topped with miso gravy. Authenticity makes everything taste good.

⊱ Day 20 ⊰

Courage:
Meeting the Other
Pilgrim with No Parents

*You've got to jump off cliffs all the time and build your
wings on the way down.*

—ANNIE DILLARD

The day my brother called to say that he was with
our father in the emergency room of Mount Sinai
Hospital, I was sitting in my living room about to eat a
piece of carrot cake. The next thing I knew, I was holding
the hand of a confused man in a hospital gown.

Earlier in the day, my father had wandered off on his
own, a creeping symptom of early onset dementia, and
he had slipped and hit his head on a concrete sidewalk.
A streetcar driver had called the ambulance that took
my father to the hospital. And then, there we were, facing the unknown. That day would be the beginning of
the death of my father, a process that ended ten weeks
later.

You need a singular kind of courage to stay within the cold and sterile walls of a hospital emergency room overnight, especially if you are in a confused mental state. On the night of my father's accident, for the first few hours my presence was simply a comfort. When I asked my dad if he wanted me to stay with him through the night, he answered by clinging onto my hand tightly. I represented a familiar anchor. And the two of us existed as the minutes ticked by. Around the fourth hour or so, my father became increasingly agitated, but because of the confused state brought on by the head injury, he was unable to communicate the cause of his discomfort. And the agitation intensified by the minute. The overworked nurses were not aware of the fact that my father's belly was ballooning up, even as I kept at them to try and uncover the source of his pain. I couldn't see his protruding stomach through his loose mint-green hospital gown, and wouldn't have thought to look there anyway. It wasn't until I pressed a male nurse to search for the cause of my dad's ongoing increasingly agonized squirms that the nurse finally thought to look at my dad's belly.

And then the nurse put a catheter in. As it turned out, my father's insufferable pain was the result of not being able to relieve himself for hours—his bladder had become over-filled with urine. That one night would introduce the subsequent sixty-nine bewildering nights for my brave father, interspersed only rarely with moments of lucidity, until the morning of his death.

<hr />

I am sitting in the dining hall when a soft presence wafts in the room. The new pilgrim is carrying a violin case. The first thing I notice about this dark-haired woman is the gentle melancholic air that surrounds her. I am drawn to her immediately and offer her a cup of hot tea. Born and raised in Japan, Taka had been touring Europe

115

performing concerts in opera houses and theaters as a featured violinist, and has come to Plum Village for a retreat between musical engagements.

I have already gotten used to the sped-up friendships that develop when one lives communally with others. Everyone has come to this sanctuary in search of their own refuge from god knows what. Banal chatting is pointless. This is the reason that after ten minutes of knowing Taka, I discover that she too has lost both her parents—her mother very recently. Unlike me, with my two brothers, Taka is without siblings or close relatives. In fact, she tells me that she knows of only a few distant relatives. Taka looks to be somewhere in her early thirties—far too young to be left with no one in the world.

Sometimes while gazing at the many different faces here, I wonder what personal battles lie behind their expressions—because carnage is certainly there. A towering, rail thin, pale monk with a gigantic hooked nose and glum look about him moderated the Dharma discussion for the pilgrims of New Hamlet earlier today. During the discussion, a pilgrim indicated that she was feeling depressed, and the pale monk responded: "Sometimes mental anguish is so bad that one simply must sit without moving for several hours, in order to just be able to function on the most basic of levels."

It is no small act of courage to embrace the pain from the past or the unknown suffering of the future, with dignity, mindfulness, and acceptance. This is what the gentle violinist, Taka, did by venturing to a monastery, and what the anguished hook-nosed monk with the mysterious past endeavored by turning monastic. It was what my father endured that first night in the hospital and each night afterward until his death. And yet many of us do not live bravely in the moment. As celebrated American journalist and playwright Fulton Oursler once wrote, "Many of us crucify ourselves between two thieves—regret for the past and fear of the future."

Tibetan Buddhist Chogyam Trungpa recognized that there are people who have a special kind of courage—one that is innately intelligent, gentle, and fearless. He called one who embodies these qualities a spiritual warrior. "Spiritual warriors can still be frightened, but even so, they are courageous enough to taste suffering, to relate clearly to their fundamental fear, and to draw out without evasion the lessons from difficulties."

Taka is a spiritual warrior.

If we didn't have fear to face, we would never have the opportunity to discover our courage, and the miraculous gems inherent in that bravery. The poet Rainer Maria Rilke said, "Our deepest fears are like dragons guarding our deepest treasure." I think of this now as I sit here with Taka. I imagine her lonely life contributing to her exquisite musical gift—the one that will immediately bring tears to my eyes, tomorrow, when she plays a Bach piece full of expert minor notes and sadness. And I think of the hook-nosed monk, the walking wounded, and wonder if the fears that seep into his aura and hang about him like an ever-present gloomy fog are masking some brilliant jewel that will be discovered as he bravely peers into the eyes of those dragons. For god's sake, it is simply an act of courage, all on its own, to give up possessions, attachments, carnal desires, favorite blue jeans, your own money, and to shave your head as a woman? Well, that's not so easy. I'll be able to go back to my lavender-scented hot baths, but there's not a tub in sight at the monastery. It's one thing to ground oneself in a lasting strength within the span of forty days as I am attempting; it's another thing entirely to live smack dab in the middle of world-class winemaking country and never touch a drop of Bordeaux to your lips. This is the discipline of a Plum Village monk.

During this morning's meditation instructions, I was asked to comprehend the link between my breath and my life—breathing in, I know I am alive. Thây has pointed to a problem that many of us have—when we breathe in, we don't *know* that we are breathing, which means that we are not being mindful—it's kind of like sleepwalking through life.

Taka places her teacup down as she finishes telling me the story of her mother's death. Her mother had died from cancer. The pilgrim's face radiates a dignified pain— she is not sleepwalking through this experience. Taka knows she is breathing. She *knows* her mother's breath has stopped. Taka has a depth of presence that is rich with courage. Her insight will expand at the monastery, I am sure of that.

Sometimes we're pushed off cliffs and forced to build wings on the way down. We have no other choice. Taka is *taking refuge*. She is looking at her suffering through wise eyes. Taka is "making good use of her suffering," as Thây so very practically says. I sense that my fellow pilgrim is building a glorious set of wide-reaching wings that will allow her to soar.

Impermanence: How To Be with Everything as It Changes

He who binds to himself a joy
Does the winged life destroy;
But he who kisses the joy as it flies
Lives in eternity's sun rise.

—WILLIAM BLAKE, "ETERNITY"

I am sitting on the floor of the Buddha Hall with Taka and her violin. My new friend is so very melancholic, yet her fragility exudes such honesty that I thoroughly enjoy the musical pilgrim's company, even as her sadness spills into me.

There are rare moments of sacred beauty in one's life. I am about to experience one of them now. My wistful friend carefully takes her violin out of its protective case and sets the sheath down beside her. The reverent manner in which Taka handles the instrument reveals her musical mastery even before she plays a single note. Taka slowly comes to her feet, brings the crafted piece of wood up to her shoulder, and tucks it under her pensive chin. Long black hair frames both her downcast eyes and the exquisite fiddle. Everything else in the room falls away from my view. Taka hasn't yet plucked a note, but the vision before me, by itself, causes a welling up of tears. And then it happens. Taka is swaying with the minor chords that touch the air in one moment and disappear the next. Through my wet eyes, her enchanting sadness multiplies with each virtuosic note. Taka is teaching me the truth of impermanence through her masterful rendition of Bach.

> What is our life but this dance of transient forms? Isn't everything always changing: the leaves on the trees . . . the seasons, the weather, the time of day . . . And what about us? Doesn't everything we have done in the past seem like a dream now? The friends we grew up with . . . the views and opinions we once held with single-minded passion. We have left them all behind.
>
> —SOGYAL RINPOCHE,
> THE TIBETAN BOOK OF LIVING AND DYING

Musical notes form and instantly vanish into thin air in this building where monks meditate, creating a memory within me as they disappear. The words on this page you are now reading, in the next instant, will only be a memory of yours.

> The cells of our body are dying . . . the expression on our face is always changing . . . what we call our basic character is only a mindstream, nothing more.
>
> —SOGYAL RINPOCHE,
> THE TIBETAN BOOK OF LIVING AND DYING

120

Today I feel melancholic joy as the minor chords of Bach penetrate my skin; tomorrow, I may feel the opposite. And then where will that sweet, sad feeling have gone?

> We are impermanent, the influences are impermanent, and there is nothing solid or lasting anywhere that we can point to.
> —SOGYAL RINPOCHE,
> THE TIBETAN BOOK OF LIVING AND DYING

The final note that Taka brings to life vibrates at length, leaving its resonant echo in my bones. The melancholic violinist completes a piece she must have played hundreds of times in the past, a musical poem that is part of her, and now part of me. With reverence, Taka places the violin back in its case, ever the devotional musician, and we walk out of the hall together like sisters. In our shared artistic experience here, and in death, we have understood each other. During our walk back to the residence of New Hamlet, we don't directly talk of death. Our kinship is based on a silent knowing.

> There would be no chance at all of getting to know death if it happened only once. But, fortunately, life is nothing but a continuing dance of birth and death, a dance of change.
> —SOGYAL RINPOCHE,
> THE TIBETAN BOOK OF LIVING AND DYING

While my father was dying, I was reading *The Tibetan Book of Living and Dying*. There is an exercise in that wise bible that helped me to accept the truth that all things change. Following the guidance of author Sogyal Rinpoche, at a particularly despairing moment, I picked up a coin and held it in my hand, with a tight fist, palm facing down. Then I imagined that the coin represented the idea at which I was grasping—my wish that my father was not dying. I saw that if I were to let go or relax my grip, I would lose the coin—that which I was clinging onto. And that's why I held onto it. I wanted my father to be healthy and alive. But there was another possibility—I could let go and yet keep hold of the coin by turning my hand over so that it faced the sky. I turned my palm up, opened my hand, and the coin still rested there. I had let go. And the coin was still mine, even with all the space surrounding it. I could still want my father to live, yet not fight the reality that he was dying.

There is a way to accept the impermanent nature of life and yet still relish and honor life, without grasping at it.

❦

I have gone to my cave and am sitting on the edge of my monastic bed, reflecting on death. For as long as I can remember, I have been fascinated by death—not that I don't fear it, but my life has unfolded in such a way that reflection upon this transition to another realm is demanded of me. As a child, I would give elaborate funerals for my various beloved rodent pets, with shoebox caskets and dandelion flower bouquets. But then, when I was seventeen years old, my mother was diagnosed with breast cancer, and I had to face the reality that death would come not only to my sweet furry pets, but also to my beloved family members.

Contemplation on death, according to Buddhists, brings a deepening awareness of renunciation. The frequent and deep reflection on death will cause an emerging out of habitual and destructive patterns of living. This letting go is said to contain both sadness and joy—and I can attest to that. There is sadness in realizing the futility of old ways of being, and joy in envisioning a future without those imprisoning habits. Sogyal Rinpoche explains:

> This is no ordinary joy. It is a joy that gives birth to a new and profound strength, a confidence, an abiding inspiration that comes from the realization that you are not condemned to your habits, that you can indeed emerge from them, that you can change, and grow more and more free. . . . Contemplating impermanence on its own is not enough. You have to work with it in your life.

Rinpoche elaborates on how to practice and apply the truth of impermanence by suggesting that we view the varying changes in our lives with understanding. That outlook will relax some of the tension within us, and surrounding all of our situations in life. This makes even very painful shifts somewhat less intense. And then we live deeper, more spacious lives.

I realize that both Taka and I have been given a gift in having to face harsh realities head on. Through the death of our loved ones, it is commanded of us that we understand the truth that all things in this world are impermanent. And yet, how very difficult it is to accept reality. Taka is now entirely alone in the world. I wonder how she is supposed to feel secure, safe, loved, included. In coming to Plum Village, Taka must knowingly, or unknowingly, also be seeking what I pursue. I wonder if that is essentially what all of us here desire—to find and nurture an eternal connection to our Home within ourselves, no matter what tragedy exists in our lives. I feel immense sadness for Taka. But Thich Nhat Hanh's wisdom leaps over my despair. In *The Heart of the Buddha's Teachings*, the Zen master writes:

It is not impermanence that makes us suffer.
What makes us suffer is wanting things to
be permanent when they are not . . . When
we know that the person we love is impermanent we will cherish our beloved all the
more. Impermanence teaches us to respect
and value every moment and all the precious things around us and inside of us . . .
We can smile because we've done our best
to enjoy every moment of our life and to
make others happy.

I have now gone from sitting to lying on my cot.
Heavy reflections have taxed my physical strength. I
remember the pale moment when my mother was told of
her breast cancer. Strangely, she had been given the news
on the phone, and I had overheard. Years after my mom's
death, I realized that because of uncertainty, of the threat
that death could have taken my mother at any moment,
I had deeply appreciated those remaining years with her,
as did my father and brothers. But I wonder now what it
would be like to wholly appreciate impermanence daily
without the fierce catalyst of a mother's life-threatening
illness. To be that awake would truly be an achievement.

The gong rings for dinner. I lift my exhausted body
and sit on the edge of my bed. It takes me ten minutes to
stand, and then another ten to walk slowly to the dining
hall. My new sister, Taka, is standing by the fireplace with
a cup of tea in one hand and her violin case in the other.
In the next moment, she has set off down the hallway,
intending to place the sacred musical instrument, the one
that had taught me the truth of impermanence, safely
away in her room, until its wisdom is needed again.

⁓ Day 22 ⁓

Earth:
I Am the Hungry Child

Earth provides enough to satisfy every man's need, but not every man's greed.

—MAHATMA GANDHI

My strict ballet training as a child drilled an impossible ideal of thinness into my mind, causing me to have an imbalanced relationship with food. I did not have an eating disorder, and perhaps I was unconsciously rebelling against my highly disciplined life as a young dancer, but sometimes I looked to food in an attempt to quash some meandering unidentified dissatisfaction.

The Eastern mystic Meher Baba decreed that: "Greed is a state of restlessness of the heart."

It is noon and one of the Sisters of New Hamlet is reading a pre-lunchtime prayer aloud. This is the same "grace before meals" that I have heard every day for twenty-one days. Today the golden words penetrate deeply: "This food is the gift of the whole universe. May we eat in mindfulness and transform our greed by eating in moderation. May we eat in a way that reduces the suffering of living beings and encourages the preservation of our planet."

In the silence that follows, I survey my plate of brown rice, steamed carrots, broccoli, and lentils in miso gravy. I glance at my neighbor, look to the serene young Sister across from me, and then my eyes travel along the table of carefully prepared dishes. In the next moment, I am filled with all the sacredness in the room.

Having a meal at a monastery is completely unlike dining in the real world. Here, you do one thing at one time. There is no reading the morning paper while drinking your tea—you just drink tea. It's hard. Take away excessive chatter, television, and countless other activities regularly juggled while eating, and you're left with, well, just eating. In fact, I sometimes see people break down in tears during a silent meal—it happened just yesterday. A fellow pilgrim, when faced with her thoughts in the quiet, must have become so over-whelmed by a sad memory or a worry that she just sat there and bawled her eyes out. Some of the pilgrims, including me, were a wee bit taken aback, but the nuns must be used to these sorts of situations, as not one of them batted a monastic eyelid.

The Buddha famously fasted for days on end in search of liberation from the suffering of old age, death, and rebirth. Many accounts say that, at one point, this brave trailblazer had survived for many weeks on only one grain of rice per day. The Buddha had been attempt-ing to squash all desire by fasting, having determined that desire itself is the cause of our suffering. And yet, he didn't find deep understanding that way.

Thich Nhat Hanh notes that the Buddha had learned firsthand that if you destroy your health, you will not be strong enough to walk the Path of Realization. He also emphasized that the opposite extreme of over-indulgence in sensual pleasures, like

126

immoderate eating, for example, is equally dangerous. The Buddha discovered and then proclaimed the *Middle Way* as the key to enlightenment. Thây describes The Buddha's Middle Way as "the way to transcend all pairs of opposites."

Each and every day here, I am reminded of the immense value in moderation. These "whisperings" guide me to a place within where I am not blown to and fro with the troubling winds of change.

I take a spoonful of dark green French lentils in the salty miso, and chew and chew and chew. I taste the legumes. I feel their texture on my tongue. Their pure, earthy scent wafts under my nose. I know I am being nourished. I have taken a smaller portion today, and am eating more slowly. I reflect on greed. There are millions of people who don't have enough to eat. But do I really *know* that? I consider this now, and it has the effect of loosening the vice grip of my emotional eating. I have taken a kind of refuge within that brings on a welcome sensation of empowerment in my choices.

Today, I stop eating before I am full.

After lunch, I pick up a newspaper and read a story predicting a future global food shortage. In many parts of the world, there will not be enough to eat for our growing population, which is predicted to increase by two to four billion people in the next forty years. This will create an extremely complex web of disastrous effects on humans, not to mention on the environment. In Africa, for example, many are so hungry that they seek their nutrition in the jungle. They kill wild animals for food, contributing to the disappearance of these necessary beasts. And this "bush meat," from various monkey species, rodents, and snakes, often contains viruses. These viruses are easily transferred to humans. There's that interconnection thing yet again. Many Africans are hunting and eating bush meat because they will otherwise starve.

I close my eyes, the newspaper falls to my lap, and I reflect again on Thây's prayer: "May we eat in a way that reduces the suffering of living beings and encourages the preservation of our planet."

In one of Thich Nhat Hanh's earlier talks, I heard him say that we should think globally *and* locally. Many say the opposite—that what you do in your own backyard ultimately influences the world. I think Thây is right— both perspectives are necessary. A deep awareness of world issues is, of course, vital knowledge to have. But beyond keeping up with current news, it is vital to personally tune in.

When you recognize that your *body* is a microcosm of the macrocosm, that is the *world*, then as you know your body, you know the world. You will be able to think globally if you are deeply aware of your own nature—but you must understand your *real* nature—not your *imagined* nature. Without proper introspection, it is so easy to confine ourselves into a self-made prison, which we mistake for the whole universe.

There is a great Buddhist tale that divulges this truth. The story is about an old frog that had lived all his life in a dank well, before being visited by a frog from the ocean. Patrul Rinpoche enlightens us:

"Where do you come from?" asked the frog in the well.

"From the great ocean," replied the frog from the ocean.

"How big is your ocean?"

"It's gigantic."

"You mean about a quarter of the size of my well here?"

"Bigger."

"Bigger? You mean half as big as my well?"

"No, even bigger."

"Is it . . . as big as this well?"

"There is no comparison."

"That's impossible! I've got to see this for myself."

So, the two frogs set off for the ocean together. When the frog from the well saw the ocean, it was in such shock, that its head exploded into pieces.

⁓⊚⊚⁓

In a French monastery, gazing through the ancient portal in my Hobbit-like abode, stretched out on my cot, and with the *International Herald Tribune* folded over me, I think of my body as the body of the starving child in Africa; and the elderly man, forced to eat bugs or bush meat to survive; and the senior nun with the limp who I see here at the monastery every day. My body is their body. With these mindful reflections I go beyond my familiar self, beyond my body. I seem to be only my breath. The defining lines of my body fade as I merge with the space.

Years ago, I had a similar kind of expansive experience while on a mountaintop in New Mexico. At twilight, after a long day of sitting meditation, I stood up to stretch my legs and began walking along the mountain, away from the many people there on retreat with me. In my view were bushy moss-green yucca shrubs, the dusky blue sky, and nothing else. Each step I took melted into the dry earth as the vastness of the sky diffused into me. In those moments, there had been no separation between what I knew of as me and everything else in my view. Within that sense of oneness I had glimpsed truth.

> My ties and ballasts leave me, my elbows rest in
>   sea-gaps,
> I skirt sierras, my palms cover continents,
> I am afoot with my vision.
> —WALT WHITMAN, "SONG OF MYSELF"

Sometimes I feel as if my head will explode from all the *stretching* going on here, but fortunately the process is gradual enough that I will probably avoid the fate of the old frog from the well.

With all that I don't know, I take a moment now and remind myself of what I do know. When I sit quietly and breathe mindfully, with the doors open and the light filtering in, a cool, blue pool of clarity appears, and answers come. And then I simply *know* that energetically, I am not *separate* from any starving child of the world, or the old man in Africa, or the feeble nun here in New Hamlet. My *still* mind knows this. I remember the Buddha's proclamation upon his awakening: "I have seen that nothing can be by itself alone, that everything has to inter-be with everything else. I have also seen that all beings are endowed with the nature of awakening."

With this insight, may I cease to possess more than I need.

⪜ Day 23 ⪝

Water:
How a Monk Washes His Face

The frog does not drink up the pond in which he lives.
—AMERICAN INDIAN PROVERB

Tonight I do not take water for granted. Tonight I know that the warm liquid flowing over my hands is a miracle.

⚹⚹⚹

This morning, during the Dharma talk, Thây had offered an intricate commentary on how he had washed his face earlier. The monk's serene visage was filled with authentic appreciation as he described in great detail the wonderful feeling of the water on his face, and his great joy in realizing the deep source of the miracle that is water:

> My fingers touched this water that had come
> from so far away, from distant mountains or
> deep in the earth, and miraculously, there it

131

was on my hands, on my face, with the simple turning of a tap. As I gently splashed this
gift over my face, I thought of all the life on
earth that exists because of water. The water
was so fresh and cold. And I was happy. My
mindfulness made me happy.

Before Thây had begun speaking, the monks and nuns
had gathered, as usual, at the front of the hall to sing their
glorious chants together as one voice, one body. It had
been mesmerizing as always, but today the mantras had
contained an even more transcendent quality. Midway
through the chant, I happened to look over at my friend
Stuart. I found the Scot completely transported, quiet tears
running down his gentle, young face. And then I listened
more deeply. In the next moment, the already resplendent
chants took me to another platform of vibratory consciousness, and I knew that the depth of my engagement with the
sounds was the reason for my feelings of transformation. To
be engaged was my responsibility. I shouldn't expect these
sacred vibrations to carry me without my willingness. A
deep focus toward these Buddhist mantras would mean a
swifter and lighter ride to the shore of freedom from past
wounds. As Stuart allowed himself to break open and fully
absorb those luminous chants, they had resonated more
deeply within him—I could see that. Stuart later told me
that he had dedicated the blessed music to his parents, who
I gathered could use a sacred blessing or two. The Scottish
pilgrim said, that upon absorbing the transporting sounds,
he had felt something shift inside of himself, and knew that
the chant had created some healing for his whole family.
    A sacred mantra, chanted with full absorption,
creates miracles.
    After Thây had spoken of the transcendental washing
of his face, he relayed a story from his youth in Vietnam.
On a school outing, hundreds of children, in small

groups, had ventured up a mountain to enjoy the natural surroundings. The young Thây had been excited about the adventure because he had heard that there was a *hermit*, a Buddhist mystery man, living and meditating in solitude up in those mountains. In their excitement, Thây and the other children in his group had climbed the mountain quickly, and by halfway, they had drunk all of their water. And then to the disappointment of Thây, this elusive hermit, this Buddha-like being, was nowhere to be found. As the children sat to eat their picnic lunches, Thây decided to explore a little further, and ventured into the wood on his own. It wasn't long before the schoolboy heard the sound of water dripping and then followed it to discover a natural well of spring water. Because this future Zen master had been so very thirsty, he was delighted to find the spring. As Thây cupped his hands into the water and brought it to his lips, he suddenly had a thought. "What if the hermit transformed himself into a well?" Upon drinking the water, the youth had felt so happy and peaceful that he no longer had the desire to meet the hermit—in the form of a person. Thây had then fallen into a deep sleep beside the well, and upon waking, he didn't know where he was. But one thing the future Zen master did know was that he had drunk the most delicious water in the world.

The young Thây never told the other children of his experience with the well, as he thought it might dilute the very powerful spiritual experience that it had been for him. But after many years and much monastic study, the monk did tell the story of the hermit and the well, because of his deep wish for everyone to meet their own hermit, within their own lifetime.

In the meditation hall this morning, I was struck by the simplicity and strength in the messages from both Stuart—to be an active participant and engage fully with the glorious chants of the Buddha in order to receive healing—and the sacred advice from Thây—to be diligent in your mindfulness, so that you don't miss out on recognizing your *own* hermit when it presents itself to you; so that your mindfulness builds not only an unwavering security and joy, but also a reverence toward the necessary elements that sustain life on earth. The well had been Thây's hermit. The sacred music was Stuart's hermit. The advice is straightforward. But, to focus consistently, to not become distracted or dispersed in one's mind—that's the challenge.

Upon viewing a transported fellow pilgrim and hearing sage commentary from a monk, my consciousness shifted. Of course water is a wonder—it is even a hermit. How could it be otherwise? Thây has a unique way of pausing for moments while speaking. And in that space, my mind processes his teachings. Nearly all life forms on earth are comprised of three-quarters water, making us all completely dependent on this liquid. I am over 70 percent water. You are over 70 percent water. I am made of this liquid, as are you. To not revere the sacred nature of water is to ignore life. Of course water is a hermit.

I have a stronger hold on my lifeline. I am pulling myself together more resolutely.

There are prayers written in multi-colored ink on plain paper and pinned on these monastery walls—in bathrooms, dining halls, kitchens, and meditation rooms. And there are specific reminders about the value of water in each room that has a tap. This evening I read this above the washroom sink: "As this water flows over my hands, may I use them well to protect our mother, the earth." I turn on the tap and hear the rush of the moving stream. My hands open underneath the warm flow. I close my eyes. My breath journeys with the sound of the water. I feel my feet on the ground. I remember the earth beneath me. This water springs from the depths of that ground. Warm liquid spills over the sides of my cupped hands. I breathe. I splash the warmth on my face. I press my fingers on my closed eyes and caress them—the water caresses them. I breathe. I cup my hands again, and feel the joy in my hands, the cleansing force there. My face is warm again, my palms pressing, my fingers massaging my eyelids. And again—more water, more warmth, on my hands, on my face. I breathe. I open my eyes. I turn the tap off and read the forest green words on the sign above the sink: "As this water flows over my hands, may I use them well to protect our mother, the earth."

As Thich Nhat Hanh said, "You may have already seen your hermit, but not recognized him. Your hermit may not be a well. It may be a rock, or a tree, or a child, or a mountain. But once you have found your hermit, you will know where to go. And you will find peace."

To follow the insightful monk and wash our faces with full attention to the value of water is to respect our home, the earth. When we go to our Home within, we recognize and value our home around us—our glorious planet. If I were to have only this one day at the monastery, all the effort it took to come to Plum Village would have been worth it.

⪻ Day 24 ⪼

Fire:
The Happy Irishman

*The burning flames of anger have parched the stream of
my being.*

—DILGO KHYENTSE RINPOCHE

I blearily look at my clock—it is 5:01 a.m., and there
they are again, frantic heels pummeling the floor of
the hallway. My neighbor has woken up and is scurrying
to the washroom. Here's the thing—there's not a chance
she would ever be late for morning meditation. "How
can she possibly move so fast at such an early hour?"
At 5:11 a.m., more shuffles. The scurrier has gone back
to her room from the washroom. I doze off. The second
gong rings; its pleasant vibrations gently rouse me from
sleep until I am fully woken up with a start by my neighbor's last dash along creaky floorboards. It's 5:15 a.m.
The enthusiastic pilgrim will arrive in the meditation hall a full fifteen minutes early. This is about the
time I usually get up, on regular days, that is—the days
when Thây is not present. When Thich Nhat Hanh is

teaching, I get my buns promptly out of bed at the first chime of the gong.

This afternoon I am walking on the damp grass of Upper Hamlet with a quick-witted, ruddy-faced Northern Irish man who is somewhere in his fifties. Good Catholic that he is, Aidan remarked a few days ago that while walking with Thây, he had felt what it might have been like to walk with Jesus. I now ask Aidan what brought him to Plum Village. He answers by telling me of his family history. One of eight children in a Belfast Catholic household, Aidan had been raised under the notion of "spare the rod, spoil the child." Aidan tells me now that he had married a woman very much like his firm-handed mother. Aidan's wife followed this harsh belief as well. But after a great deal of turmoil in the household, Aidan had begun to question his and his wife's method of raising their children. His wife hadn't wanted to soften their child-rearing approach, and that had led to endless disagreements and conflict. Aidan's marriage difficulties had triggered anger within him, and that torrid pit had deepened over a number of years, until he would blow up at even the slightest provocation. Aidan described his anger to me: "It was like a flame on a stove ready to explode at any moment if anything fueled it. I could see that my hot temper was way out of control and causing great distress to myself, my family, and everything around me." Aidan told me that he knew something had to change.

As we continue our walk on the grounds of the monks' residences, Aidan smiles and says that Thich Nhat Hanh's book *Anger* changed his life. After reading Thây's guidance on how to manage this destructive emotion, Aidan began to accept and care for his feelings of rage. Following the techniques in the book, the man from Belfast had visualized this hot emotion at his belly. Through mindfulness, the Irishman would then accept and cradle his anger, like a hurt child. Embracing his negativity, Aidan accepted and validated those feelings, which then naturally led to compassion for himself. "Soon," Aidan says, "I was able to mentally turn that fire down to just a pilot light."

I have often heard Thây say that we mustn't suppress our negative emotions. If difficult feelings arise, we must embrace them with mindfulness. "Until we recognize anger as anger, it will push us around." Only through mindfulness will we develop compassion and understanding for ourselves. To illuminate this teaching, Thây often gives the example of a mother, who upon hearing her baby cry, immediately goes to the baby, picks her up, and embraces her with love. The mother doesn't ignore the baby, especially when that baby is upset. And, even though the mother doesn't necessarily know why her baby is crying, her mindful embrace will be felt by the child, and will soothe the child. So, like a crying baby, cradled with acceptance and love, our negativity will lose its staying power—the crying will stop and compassion will arise when we embrace ourselves with care. We don't even need to be aware of why we are feeling those negative emotions. Thây emphasizes that, with attentiveness and practice, afflictions then descend back down into the depths of our mind, into what Buddhists refer to as our store consciousness, where they lie dormant and unable to do any damage.

Aidan and I are now strolling quietly together on this cool afternoon in the open French countryside. I think back on Vanna and the fateful day of the French translation. This fellow pilgrim had hurled vicious words within the sacred walls of the Buddha Hall, stunning me into silence. Vanna—the one who waters my negative seeds of anger and frustration. I realize now that I haven't been embracing those difficult feelings with understanding, and thus they have become sticky. Even the sight of Vanna causes the horrible feelings to reappear. Just like Aidan, whose wife had triggered his dark emotions to rise, causing him much distress, I have let Vanna cause me a lot of grief. I have not developed compassion toward myself, let alone toward Vanna.

Of course, all of us have these seeds of affliction, like anger, just as we also have seeds of joy, compassion, and love within us. The cool-headed Irishman has now learned how to recognize and embrace his pain and difficult feelings with mindfulness and awareness, so that those emotions become very weak and fall back down away from the forefront of his mind. I think of Aidan's refined ability now, and Thây's advice that we mustn't suppress any of our emotions. I think of my tendency to do just that with my difficult feelings—push them away rather than embrace them with understanding. Today I see the possibility of a new and compassionate relationship with my challenging emotions, and that in and of itself is a joyful awakening.

My new Irish friend has become what Thây sublimely calls "the gardener of his garden." The Buddhist monk describes mind consciousness as the gardener carefully tilling the soil in the depths of the mind, nurturing the seeds of joy and love, in the garden that is store consciousness. Mindfulness cultivates the wholesome, joyful seeds to blossom, and that same mindfulness encourages any unwholesome, afflictive seeds to return back down to store consciousness, where they can't do any damage.

The Lotus Sutra, a discourse presented by the Buddha toward the end of his life, contains a passage stating that mindfulness can transform the fires that are about to burn us into a cool, clear lotus lake. In *The Heart of the Buddha's Teachings*, Thây elaborates, "If our mind has craving, anger, and harming, we are like a house on fire. If craving, anger, and harming are absent from our minds, we produce a cool, clear, lotus lake."

The Irishman who had been like a house on fire, consumed by uncontrolled, wild anger, now looks a wee bit melancholic but peaceful as he tells me that his marriage did end. But because Aidan had discovered how to work with mindfulness in his life, he had improved his relationships with his children and now ex-wife. Aidan tells me that he plans to introduce his children to Plum Village and to the teachings of Thich Nhat Hanh.

The ruddy-faced man from Belfast is spirited and full of pluck, a most stimulating and interesting walking companion. To embody peace does not equal dullness or inertia. To be peaceful is to be vital and truly alive. I can see Aidan knows this.

ᕮ Day 25 ᕲ

Air:
How a Fat Suitcase
Taught Me to Surrender

Materialism coarsens and petrifies everything, making everything vulgar, and every truth false.

—Henri-Frédéric Amiel

There are two senior monks and two senior nuns sitting like resolute Buddhas at the front of the Dharma Hall of Upper Hamlet. All four of them emanate a refined Buddhist sophistication. Some of the visiting pilgrims have submitted questions for this panel of monastics to answer. Around two hundred of us sit here quietly. A Sister reads the first question aloud: "How does one develop non-attachment, and truly let go in life?" The nun pauses, and then slowly lifts her graceful face to say, "Letting go of ideas is much harder than letting go of possessions." She then says, "Letting go of possessions is a good practice for letting go of ideas." The exquisite Sister says that at Plum Village,

141

the monastics change rooms each year so they will not become attached to a particular room or roommate. She then adds, "*Mind your own business* truly means: look deep inside of yourself. Do not be concerned with what other people are doing. Pay attention only to what you are doing."

For my journey to France, I had packed two large suitcases with all the items I would *need* for my four-month stay. I had favorite clothes for all occasions, books, treasured organic body products, and various sundries. Here's what happened: Both bags were overweight, forcing me to pay the airport's heavy load transport fees. Then, lugging these cases through the escalator-challenged Parisian subways proved next to impossible. To say I was weighed down is putting it mildly. Luckily, a month into my journey one bright moment arose. A Canadian friend came to visit me in Paris and agreed to take one of my cases back to Toronto. My savior! But the remaining bag was stuffed to the max and I quickly realized that my possessions had become more than just a physical burden. By the time I reached Plum Village that bloated bag of stuff had left me mentally unsettled.

"Letting go of possessions is a good practice for letting go of ideas." I wish I had that sage advice while I was packing those bags.

The Buddha said, "Attachment to views, attachment to ideas, attachment to perceptions are the biggest obstacle to the truth." In his book *The Art of Power*, Thich Nhat Hanh explains:

> It's like when you climb a ladder. When you
> get to the fourth rung, you may think you are
> on the highest step and cannot go higher, so
> you hold on to the fourth rung. But in fact
> there is a fifth rung; if you want to get to it,

you have to be willing to abandon the fourth rung. Ideas and perceptions should be abandoned all the time, to make room for better ideas and truer perceptions. This is why we must always ask ourselves, "Am I sure?"

During his Dharma talk this morning, before the question and answer period with the panel of monastics, Thây had talked of the necessity of "burning our notions"—these ideas of ours that hold us back from seeing the truth of reality, especially our unexamined views of birth and death: "Your nature is the nature of no birth, no death. You are a continuation." Thây then poured some tea into a cup and said that he was "pouring a cloud." This beautiful phrase demonstrates that a cloud cannot die. A cloud simply continues on in another form; in this case, it has become water for the tea. "We can't see the cloud as a 'sign,' but it is certainly there in the tea." Buddhists call this *signlessness*, and along with *emptiness* and *aimlessness*, it is one of the *Three Doors of Liberation* through which we become liberated from fear, confusion, and sadness. Thây continued on, "We are like the cloud. We do not die. We simply continue on in other forms." Deep-thinking Buddhists transcend the ideas of birth and death.

I am gazing at the sculpted face of a Vietnamese nun who appears much younger than her age. Gazing at her smooth, bald head shining in the light of the meditation hall as she repeats her dictum, I wonder again if I am attached to my long, blonde hair. I take a piece and twist it around my index finger. I am very fond of my hair—it feels like a possession not unlike my favorite clothes or jewelry. Would letting go of my hair liberate my mind?

The ageless nun continues on. She is attempting to help all of us understand *how* to let go, not only of material possessions, but in every aspect of our lives.

If you live deeply now, you will heal from
your past. Learn how to write your happiness.
What do you see, hear, and feel? Feel the
movement of your hand as you write. Your
hand, the paper, pen, and movement are all
one. No 'one' is writing. Write a letter to
your five year-old self. Then, compassion will
naturally arise within you. If you do this with
everything, you will transform your pain into
compassion. Walk with yourself as a five-
year-old, eat with yourself as a five-year-old,
care for the child within you. If you can do
this, you will develop love and understanding for every aspect of your being.

Sometimes I lie perfectly still on the cot, eyes fixed
on the quiet ceiling in my Hobbit cave, and ponder the
many things that I will once again have to lug around
France after I leave the monastery. And I often think,
"What immense freedom a monastic life contains."
A monk doesn't own a thing—not even hair to take care
of. Frankly, it must be somewhat of a relief.

There are so many worldly things to want. Satisfaction
doesn't last long, however. Living amongst happy, posses-
sion-free nuns shines a spotlight on this truth. Here, I find
myself overjoyed as I slowly get rid of my belongings, using
up the many products I have brought from Canada; my
various soaps, shampoos, and creams. Tossing yet another
bottle into the recycling bin is a cause for celebration. It
means one less thing to cart around France.

In Eastern yogic teachings, it is said that when we redi-
rect ourselves away from wanting things, we instead desire
attachment to real, living, breathing creatures. Our misunderstanding celebrates those who acquire and own vast
amounts of things in this world. We are deemed successful,

and therefore worthy of respect based on the simple fact that we managed to work enough hours, to accumulate enough wealth, to then have the means to acquire loads of stuff. How is sucking the life out of the planet admirable? It is a deeply flawed way of thinking and living. This truth becomes amplified living in Plum Village.

Later this night, I find the Sister who had sung the gentle lullaby that had elicited memories of my mother. I have been looking for her because I want to inquire about the Buddhist head-shaving ritual. Sister Prune is sitting on a wooden stool, low to the ground, in the coldest room of the monastery—the dishwashing area. The young French nun is patiently cracking walnuts with a small rock, removing the shell, and placing the plump pieces of light brown nut-flesh one by one into a silver bowl. I could have just walked into a film scene portraying life in some eighteenth-century French monastery. I bring a second small stool close to the patient nun, crouch down, and ask if I may help. Sister Prune looks up to say yes, her freckled nose crinkling as she smiles. I am getting used to patiently undertaking repetitive tasks here at the monastery, but as I watch this Sister's method of cracking these nuts, it looks torturously slow—I mean, really, there are more efficient tools to free kernels from their shells. I enjoy Sister Prune's company, though, so it's easy for me to sit, crack, and talk with her. I take a little rock and cautiously hit a nut on the floor. It takes five knocks before I am able to hit the thing with just the right amount of force to split the shell open without demolishing the nut-flesh—not too hard but not too soft. "Just like life," I think. "We have to apply the right amount of pressure."

I ask Sister Prune about the moment she took her vows to become a Buddhist nun. "It was beautiful," she proclaims. I ask the freckle-faced nun to describe how and when her head had been shaved. I didn't think it was possible for Sister Prune's face to soften even more than its usual gentle expression. The childlike nun tells me that Thich Nhat Hanh and all of her fellow Sisters, dressed in their formal saffron orange robes overlaying their everyday brown ones, were present at her ordination. After reciting vows and sutras, Thây had ceremoniously clipped a segment of hair from the willing girl's head, and then left the room. All the Sisters then continued shaving off the newly ordained nun's curls as all of them sang lovely songs. "There was much joy, laughter, and love," She says. "It was the best day of my life." As the Sister speaks, I remember a movie in which Natalie Portman has her head shaved—crying the whole time, as if the loss of her hair had been complete torture.

I found out much later that while an aspirant, before Sister Prune had taken her vows, her older American Sister of New Hamlet, Sister Pine, used to love squeezing through her fingers the dark, thick curls of the soon to be bald-headed French Buddhist nun. Sister Pine told me that Sister Prune used to have the most lustrous and beautiful head of hair. While Sister Pine was telling me this, I experienced a fleeting moment of sadness for the loss of dark curls on a young French girl's head, but in Sister Pine's voice, there was only freedom and joy.

Amidst the ladles and pans and gigantic pots that hold one hundred cups of soup in this monastic workroom, I sit on a three-legged stool, crouched over a pile of cracked nutshells, with a small, grey rock in my hands, hearing about a French girl's delightful journey toward the Buddha, one in which she not only willingly let go of her gorgeous curls, but also quite happily surrendered her possessions. I bet Sister Prune can also release ideas, these stifling notions so many of us mistakenly hold.

I think back on this morning's panel of scholarly monastics. All of them had conveyed the value in truly letting go, not only through their insightful advice, but also in their appearance, which emitted freedom, light, and happiness. On my next trip, I will be sure to leave the fat suitcase behind.

∾ Day 26 ∾

Reverence:
The Willem Dafoe
Lookalike Monk

Always and in everything, let there be reverence.

—CONFUCIUS

I stand up from my seat on the floor of the meditation hall just as a striking monk walks by. A Sister introduces us. Here I am with the American monk. He looks like a young Willem Dafoe. A few days later, I mention this to him, and he doesn't know who this famous actor is, which I find refreshing and wonderful—especially since this famous actor lookalike monk has been living within the film-free walls of the monastery for only one year. I launch into a series of accolades for Thây. The monk heartily agrees. He then proclaims, "Mary, it's wonderful you are here!"

I have just met the monk who will change the way I think about men.

The Dafoe lookalike monk is around forty years old, with shining blue eyes and a brilliant mind. When he tells me that he has a PhD in electrical engineering, I am initially surprised that he now lives in a monastery. I ask him why he became a monk. Even as I pose the question, I know that intelligent people are drawn to the Buddha's intricate and vast teachings. The monk says that as a young boy he had had a great interest in Christianity. That spiritual curiosity evolved toward the teachings of the Buddha.

Next, I surprise myself. I have known this monk for exactly five minutes, and he is a monk, yet I feel so comfortable with him that I easily inquire: "Do you miss having a partner?" He replies that he doesn't. He goes on to say that he had never been drawn to having his own children, and that being a typical family man wasn't for him. But he openly offers: "Of course I used to enjoy sex. But I had no choice whether or not to become a monk." He says that living the life of a celibate Buddhist just makes a lot of sense to him. He tells me that the practical aspects of having a partner—the hard work inherent in personal relationships—restricts the time needed to advance on the path of gathering wisdom. At the same time, he acknowledges that for some, having a partner is also a legitimate path to deep understanding.

But here's what catches my attention. This respectful Brother is so completely present while speaking with me that I am carried deeply into the moment with him. There is no dispersion in my mind. The monk is standing directly facing me, at eye level, in a solid yet relaxed way. His eyes don't leave mine, yet there is only openness and reverence in them. There is no thought of "Have we talked long enough? What is she thinking about me?" The familiar tension between opposite sexes doesn't exist between us. Our conversation is easy and fluid, yet utterly stimulating. Neither of us leads it to an end. After a while, we simply turn together, and walk in silence. I feel an unfamiliar kind of intimacy with this man-turned-monk—an affection that is deep and respectful. We have let ourselves be seen by each other—simply because we have found ourselves together. I find this pure recognition and openness heartbreaking because it is not a more common way of relating.

> The Buddha compared the universe to a vast net woven of a countless variety of multi-faceted, brilliant jewels. Each jewel reflects in itself every other jewel in the net, and is also one with every other jewel.
>
> —Sogyal Rinpoche,
> The Tibetan Book of Living and Dying

I say goodbye to the monk and continue walking on the grounds of Upper Hamlet amidst these grapes of many a bottle of Bordeaux. It seems to me that reverence for everything in the universe will come about if I truly know that all life is in this interconnected, interdependent lattice-work that the Buddha so beautifully described. I am asked to remember the truth of inter-being every day. The more I understand this one truth, the more I will embody every other one of my insights. I sense this now. Interconnection is a deep insight. As Thây has stated countless times, the Buddha's proclamation upon his awakening was this: "I have seen that nothing can be by itself alone; everything has to inter-be with everything else." As Thây emphasizes, the Buddha came to this insight through deep meditative practice, not through the intellect. I scan my eyes along the horizon of the countryside. Practicing the Buddha's teachings and applying them to life is the only way to advance wisdom. There is no confusion in wisdom. There is no fear in wisdom. Confusion is in a tight embrace with fear.

Day twenty-six. I am the carpenter of the Home that is my self. And the construction site is starting to look more organized over here.

Thây emphasizes that the father and son are not separate. When Thây used this example today to illuminate the teaching of inter-being, I thought of a cousin of mine in England who had cut off all contact with his father. That separation had carried on for many years, through his father's ongoing degenerative illness, and right up until the day his father died. He didn't attend his father's funeral. In fact, my cousin didn't even know of his father's death until another uncle of ours tracked down my cousin to let him know that his father had died. I don't know what had initially caused the rift between the two of them—we grew up in separate countries and had only met a few times but I knew that there'd been a divorce between his parents. Things must have been very strained, as my cousin took the symbolic step of changing his surname to that of his mother's. He must have wanted to forget altogether that his father was a part of him.

It is not possible to disown anyone. Thây has presented the Buddha's insight of inter-being in a way that makes this very clear to me. And what a strange word. No one *owns* anyone. But even to disavow or reject another—this is also futile. The illusion that we can dismiss the connection we have with our family members seems to me to be exactly that—an illusion. We are obviously linked, and not only by blood. My cousin must have thought that escape was possible if he cut off all contact with his father. I wonder now, years after his father's death, if my cousin still thinks the same way. I had always liked this uncle of mine. I also know that my cousin's father had, for many years, carried a great sadness with him, because of the physical separation between him and his only son.

In Thây's Dharma talk this morning, he said, "All suffering disappears with Right View . . . You contain your father. Your father contains you. When you see that you come from your father, then you know that you *are* your father. This is the inter-being/non-dualistic way of understanding the world." He then talked of five types of concentrations that the Buddha recommended we use as shovels to dig the ground of our mind: interdependence, emptiness, inter-being, impermanence, and non-self.

Many Buddhist traditions have used the metaphor of a wave in an ocean of water to illustrate that we do not have a distinct identity or self in the world. I like the way Sogyal Rinpoche explains this in *The Tibetan Book of Living and Dying*:

> Think of a wave in the sea. Seen in one way, it seems to have a distinct identity—a beginning and an end, a birth and a death. Seen in another way, the wave itself doesn't really exist, but is just the behavior of water, empty of any separate identity but full of water. So, when you really think about the wave, you come to realize that it is something made temporarily possible by wind and water, and is dependent on a set of constantly changing circumstances. You also realize that every wave is related to every other wave.

In this passage are the Five Concentrations—a wave's existence is dependent on the circumstances (wind and water). The wave has a certain kind of behavior, but is still water and therefore it is empty of any separate identity—this is, non-self. The wave is obviously linked or interconnected to all the other waves and therefore has the nature of inter-being. And that one wave will not last forever—it comes and goes—its nature is impermanence.

Thây notes that we should not be afraid of emptiness. In his book, *no death, no fear*, he sheds light on this vital

151

Buddhist tool: ". . . emptiness just means the extinction of ideas. Emptiness is not the opposite of existence. It is not nothingness or annihilation." To help us understand emptiness, Thây had used the metaphor of two glasses. He had asked us to visualize one glass with some tea in it, and a second glass with no tea. Then Thây said, "To be empty or not empty, a glass has to be there. So, emptiness does not mean non-existence. The emptiness of the glass does not mean the non-existence of the glass. The glass is there but it is empty."

In *The Heart Sutra*, the Bodhisattva of compassion, Avalokitesvara, is instructing the monk Sariputra on how to perfect wisdom. Avalokitesvara proclaims a most celebrated Buddhist paradox: "Form is emptiness. Emptiness is form."

After lunch this afternoon, I wander over to a young man standing by himself. Twenty-one-year-old Tom looks typically Californian, blonde and blue-eyed with a surfer dude look about him and a quiet but strong presence. We walk together. Tom tells me of his aspirations to become a monk. My initial reaction is one of surprise. For older people, I understand this reasoning—they have already lived a full life, perhaps had a family, and then have become tired of the hustle and bustle of life in the so-called "real" world. I even understand the choice of the fortyish Willem Dafoe lookalike monk. He is twice the age of the young Tom. There are many young Vietnamese monastics, of course, but for them it is a strong cultural tradition. So why would a twenty-one-year-old, good-looking, smart, American youth want to become a monk?

I find that I like the young aspirant. I like him very much. He is well-spoken, honest, and reflective. Before long, I work up the courage to ask Tom why he doesn't want a "normal" life filled with girlfriends, football, and pizza. He tells me that as a young teenager, he had become intensely curious about spiritual pursuits when he read a book on meditation, tried it, and then became consumed with the practice. Tom says that at first, he probably practiced incorrectly and had some strange experiences attempting to teach himself. He then decided to seek out guide. It wasn't long before he came across the teachings of Buddhism, and those of Thich Nhat Hanh in particular. And now here he is, all the way from his home in Missouri, walking on the grounds of that very monk's monastery in France.

We have finished our walk, and now sit together in the brilliant sunlit garden of Upper Hamlet, the majestic temple spire reflecting in the clear pond of lotuses before us. I become bolder with my questions. I have to ask Tom about sex because, my god, this young, attractive man must have desires. Tom's answer is plain. His childhood had been stable, with two loving parents. He assures me that no particular experience had damaged him in any way during his formative years. He then tells me that it simply means more to him to commune with a higher energy than to dabble in meaningless pursuits. Tom says that he finds the contemplative life ultimately more satisfying than just coasting along without deep reflection.

We sit in silence. I throw a pebble into the still lotus pond. The ripples caused by the stone shiver along the water's moss-green surface. The small waves merge together so that I can't see them as distinct after a few moments. The American man and the Canadian woman appear to be different—unique ripples in the pond—but the deeper truth is that ultimately they are interconnected and of the same basic nature. They touch each other, which means that they are each affected by the nature of the other. This insight carries responsibility. In this moment, I know that everything I think, say, and do will, like a ripple in the water here, create endless interconnected ripples. And the exact size and texture of those repercussions will be unknowable to me. My eyes drink in the lotus pond. There are countless "Toms" in the world, yet all these life forms are linked to me in some way.

Every wave is related to every other wave.

In *The Heart of the Buddha's Teachings*, Thây advises: "Liberation is the ability to go from the world of signs to the world of true nature. We need the relative world of the wave, but we also need to touch the water, the ground of our being . . . We shouldn't allow relative truth to imprison us and keep us from touching absolute truth. Looking deeply into relative truth, we penetrate the absolute. Relative and absolute truths inter-embrace."

The ripples in the pond have stilled, and I think about the sex drive of the average twenty-one-year-old man. I ask Tom how he manages to control his natural sexual impulses. His answer comes without pause. If he sees an attractive form, he simply averts his eyes and focuses on the trees or the nature in front of him until his desire diminishes. He says that this brings him back into an expansive feeling of union with everything and beyond the specific, immediate primal urge.

To me, Tom is discovering reverence; the Willem Dafoe lookalike monk, in his very way of being, emits this devotion. The monastic path is not for me, I know this, but to be truly respectful of all people, and all life, to gain the insight of inter-being to the extent that it causes me to honor every jewel in the interconnected web of jewels that is this universe, that would be magnificent.

154

❦ Day 27 ❧

Engagement:
Looking Suffering in the Eye

*The difference between what we do and what we are
capable of doing would suffice to solve most of the world's
problems.*

—MAHATMA GANDHI

My father's mental capacities had already been deteri-
orating because of early onset dementia well before
the fall that caused a subdural hematoma—bleeding in
his head. The physician described my father's brain as "a
shrunken mass swimming around in a skull." There are
few resources for an aging, impaired brain to heal from a
serious trauma.

It's day twenty-seven of the retreat, and my violinist
friend Taka is sitting a few rows over in the Buddha Hall.
Melancholy hovers over her, but she is rapt, absorbing a
Zen master's counsel. Taka is looking her own pain straight

in the eye without self-pity. My companion in parental loss has caused me to reflect on my father's passing.

The days leading up to my father's death had been full of mental anguish. The whole family had been suffering, but my father's pain must have been horrendous. To have moments of lucidity eclipsed by long periods of confusion, and all the while unable to feed himself, walk, use the washroom on his own, or express himself coherently, must have been torture. My father would battle the nurses every time they attempted to bathe or change him—I mean really push them away. It would always take two people—one family member holding my father's hands down, and then a nurse working as quickly as possible to administer hygiene. The whole of my family looked into the eyes of suffering from the day of my father's accident and every day until his death. If the torment had carried on much longer than seventy days, I don't know how we would have coped seeing our frail and beloved father in agony every day.

"Do not avoid contact with suffering or close your eyes before suffering. Do not lose awareness of the existence of suffering in the life of the world. Find ways to be with those who are suffering, including personal contact, images, and sound. By such means, awaken yourself and others to the reality of suffering in the world."

Today during his Dharma talk, Thich Nhat Hanh is talking about this precept on suffering that he had created during the Vietnam War.

In the *Shambhala Sun*, Andrea Miller described the ways in which Thich Nhat Hanh had found to be with those who were suffering during the Vietnam War.

In seven boats filled to the brim with food, Thich Nhat Hanh and a small team of volunteers rowed up the Thu Bon River, going high into the mountains, where soldiers were

156

shooting at each other and the air reeked of dead bodies. The team was without mosquito netting or potable water, and, despite the icy winds, they slept and took their meals of plain rice in their boats. Under these harsh conditions, Nhat Hanh who had previously contracted malaria and dysentery, suffered a recurrence of both.

Miller continued describing the conditions in South Vietnam in 1964:

After days of heavy rain in the region, gorges had overflowed so quickly that it was impossible to escape the floods, leaving more than 4,000 people dead and thousands of homes washed away. The whole country mobilized to provide relief but the victims in the conflict areas were suffering the most and no one—except Nhat Hanh and his team—was willing to risk getting caught in the crossfire of the war to go to their aid . . . Thich Nhat Hanh and his brave team did not discriminate between those that were suffering. They provided food and aid to wounded soldiers on both sides.

When the 2004 Asian Tsunami hit, I was meditating in a countryside Buddhist retreat center, very close to the Indian coastal city of Chennai. In this meditation course, I had met an Australian woman. Post-tsunami, the two of us had been offered refuge by a generous American woman living and working as a teacher in India. That night, the three of us had slept in the American's apartment, a half a mile from the ocean. There had been warnings of a secondary gigantic wave, and the American, while generous and thoughtful, hadn't mentioned that she lived so close to the Chennai coast. There was no second wave, thankfully. That next morning, glued to the TV news, we got a sense of the immensity of the disaster.

Then she said it. The Australian announced that she was not going to let anything impact her travel plans, and that she had decided to stick with her carefully prepared itinerary, pre-tsunami. Something about the way she said it has stayed with me all these years. It wasn't that she lacked compassion; it had just seemed too disorienting and unsettling for her to acknowledge that masses of dead people were floating in the ocean, just outside of our apartment door. After some days, as soon as local transport started up again, the Australian left to continue her travels. The American who had given us refuge and another local teacher both did a lot of work to help the orphaned children of the deceased fisherman of South Chennai. I was somewhat able to help them with their project.

Upon hearing the story of Thich Nhat Hanh risking his health and life by venturing into the battle territory of Vietnam and falling deathly ill, I remembered my time in India. After the tsunami, local people went to the coast to gather the dead bodies. Assistance was needed, but only trained health professionals had been appealed to. Regardless, many unskilled people had volunteered. There had also been talk of outbreaks of typhoid, malaria, and other diseases associated with rotting corpses. That was enough to keep me away. The thought of highly infectious diseases kept me from plunking myself in the middle of dead bodies.

In the monastery of the monk who knows how to look suffering in the eye, I now wonder what it's like to be exceptionally compassionate and fearless, as Thich

Nhat Hanh and his team had been when they voluntarily went deep into the conflict of the Vietnam War, and then bravely risked their own lives to save those that surely would have died otherwise. They were engaged with life, active and unafraid, yet not reckless. This is a balance, yes, but sitting in this Buddhist place of worship today, with the monk who soldiered through the Vietnam War, I understand that I am capable of much more.

After the Vietnamese monk's talk today, I feel less afraid. If we ourselves are full of fear, how can we venture out into the world? I connect the dots. This enduring, solid self that I am building here within the monastery's wise walls does not contain fear. And this strong self desires to engage with life courageously because there's no risk of internal collapse. I see this in Thây—no matter what, there is no danger that his foundation would ever collapse—it's built on far too much wisdom.

At the end of the day, I recall a letter given to my father from a leading cancer research organization that he had volunteered with after my mother's death. My brother Iain found the letter after our dad's passing. The letter of thanks contained the wish that my father be cloned, so valuable was his service to the organization. The courageous fully engage with life.

☞ Day 28 ☜

Grace:
The Beauty of a Dying Man, a
Gliding Monk, and a Unique Baby

Everything has beauty but not everyone sees it.

—CONFUCIUS

In the nights before my father's death, I used to sleep on a mattress on the floor beside his hospital bed. My brothers were with our father during the daytime. I had volunteered for the night shift because I knew that people are more likely to die during these late hours, and I wanted to be there when it happened. On one of those nights, I had sensed that my father might be about to die, and then quickly realized that I was not mentally prepared for his passing. That night I had taken my father's hand in mine, his consciousness long since altered as he slowly slipped from this world, and I asked him to please stay a little longer. I was not ready for him to leave.

A few days later, it was time.

I have always thought of the smooth passing of my father as his most graceful gift to his family. It was just past 9:00 a.m. I was kneeling by my father's side while my brother Iain stood bravely in the corner of the hospital room, unable to bring himself closer to his beloved dying father. My devoted eldest brother, David, was making his hurried way to the hospital. In the next moments, our father's breathing and face color began to change, signaling his move toward death. I carefully removed the IV from his arm, rolled him very gently onto his right side, and sharpened my concentration to help him pass. I was following the guidelines from *The Tibetan Book of Living and Dying* to help my father transition smoothly.

The *Sleeping Lion* is the posture the Buddha was in when he died. His left hand rested on his left thigh, and his right hand was under his chin, closing his right nostril. The right side of the body contains subtle energy channels referred to by Buddhists as the karmic wind of delusion, which one wants to block before death. Thus, positioning a dying person on their right side will close off these channels and help the person recognize the radiant clarity of the nature of their mind, often called "ground luminosity," or "clear light." Then the consciousness can more easily leave the body through the top of the head. *The Tibetan Book of Living and Dying* explains:

> Our consciousness, which is mounted on a "wind" and so needs an aperture through which to leave the body, can leave through any one of nine openings. The route it takes determines exactly which realm of existence we are to be reborn in. When it leaves through the crown of the head, we are reborn, it is said, in a pure land (the state of

mind in which you are liberated from your suffering), where we can gradually proceed toward enlightenment.

⁂

Trained in classical ballet, I have danced all my life. I've seen many of the best dancers in the world perform astounding artistic feats, but it is here in a Zen monastery in France that I am witness to the embodiment of grace. I am sitting in the third row of the Buddha Hall in New Hamlet watching Thây's trademark glide along the floor. The monk's hands are moving through the air as if they *are* the air. It is evident that Thây is present and awake to the depth of freedom within each instant thus he is transcendent. Observing the grace, I become transfixed by the Zen teacher's luminosity, and am elevated—free from my troubles for these precious moments. It seems as if the weightless monk is walking on water—so fluid are his steps. And truly, I have never seen a more graceful human hand.

In the presence of Thây I now become more acutely aware of my own self. How is my hand holding this pen? Is there tension while I write? How am I sitting, breathing? What is on my mind? Is my body relaxed? Watching Thây spurs on this mental checklist. When I am deeply conscious of the quality of the moment, grace descends upon me. Sitting in front of this gentle monk, I feel immense relief.

There is a story from the teachings of Taoism that I love. The teaching is on the recognition that there is no self-consciousness in the newborn child. But as we age, the mind starts to wander into self-images. We start to think, "Should I do this? Is this movement right?" We lose the immediacy of the moment. A modern translation of the *Tao Te Ching* by Stephen Mitchell elaborates on this observation by noting that, as self-consciousness develops, the muscles become less supple, less like the world. But the young child is pure fluidity. The child isn't aware of any separation, and thus all its movements are spontaneous, alive, whole, and perfect. If an adult body becomes truly supple, though, there is a quality to its movement that the child doesn't have—a texture of experience, a fourth dimension of time. In the movement of an eighty-four-year-old's hand, we can see that "Yes, that hand has lived"—it is resonant with experience. In the movement of a child's hand there is a sense of just arriving—it is pristine and innocent and delightful. But a truly supple adult movement is awesome because all of life is included in it.

Some months after I returned home from the monastery, I visited a friend of mine and his newborn baby. My friend has an inherited genetic condition called Syndactyly, which causes him to have misshapen fingers. I wondered if the baby would also have the same condition. My friend happily greeted me at the door to his house, and I followed him up the stairs to the living room. There, sleeping soundly in a cradle, was his sweet baby. I peeked in at the little one. He had soft, dark hair, glowing skin, and a perfectly cherubic face. As I reached out to gently stroke his head, I saw his tiny curled hand up by his pink cheek. He had the same fused fingers as his father.

Thich Nhat Hanh teaches that if you look for ugly, that is what you will see. But if you look for beauty, that grace will reveal itself to you.

It was easy for me to see the beauty of the child in front of me because children are inherently lovely, pristine, and innocent. Even this baby's tiny, misshapen hands seemed perfect to me. In the presence of this child, was evidence of Thây's teaching that opposites inter-are. Beauty and ugly exist together. It's just not always obvious.

My dying father, the gliding, eighty-four-year-old monk, and the gentle newborn babe each radiate grace. Grace heals the world. There is far too much tension and rigidity all around us, and that tough energy is damaging. Those who emanate beauty and grace smooth the jagged edges of life.

⌐ Day 29 ⌐

Breath:
How Come We Take Our
Breath for Granted?

And God is always there, if you feel wounded.
He kneels over this earth like a divine medic,
And His love thaws the holy in us.

       —SAINT TERESA OF AVILA

Sixty-nine days after my father's accident, his breath
ceased altogether.

People with brain injuries who are close to death
often experience an unusual change in their breath patterns called Cheyne-Stokes respiration. The morning my
father was to pass, my brother Iain and I watched our
dad's breathing cycles become increasingly frequent and
shallow, followed by excruciatingly long pauses with
no inhalations or exhalations. Then suddenly, a breath
would come, slowly at first, and then choppy and shallow
for several rounds, followed again by a gaping standstill.

And on it went until the final exhalation that took all of our breaths away.

On November 22, 1991 at 1:30 a.m. I was sitting at the hospital bedside of my mother, sorrowfully watching her stifled breaths chop in and out of her still young and beautiful face. Then, in one instant, her breath stopped. A vein on her neck pulsed three times, and she was gone.

We possess the deluded thought that we will always breathe. We do not honor this potent energy responsible for life. If you stopped breathing, in about three minutes you would be dead.

There is a speedy, wee Irish woman here at New Hamlet. I say "speedy" because she regularly goes out for hour-long walks that verge on running. I say wee, because she is exactly four-foot-eleven inches tall. Unlike the Sisters, Mona tells me that she will absolutely rip her hair out if she is forced to walk at the snail's pace of a nun. I like her pluck. Today, I am walking back to New Hamlet from a visit to town with the pixie-like pilgrim.

And . . . we're off! The pixie is miles shorter than me, yet I am struggling to keep her pace. We are booting it back to the monastery. Any faster, and we would be running. Somehow, Mona manages to speak words. "There's no sore ass like your own sore ass." Of course I think this means that her bum muscles are in pain because she bloody well exercises them all the time. But then, she tells me that she misses Ireland, and that this is a famous Irish saying meaning "there's no place like home." I then tell Mona about another of my walks a few days ago with two French women who looked to be somewhere in their fifties. The three of us had been walking along the circular path surrounding the grounds of New Hamlet, and I, feeling happy and strange, plunked myself in the middle of them, hooked each of my arms through one of theirs, and began singing, "We're off to see the wizard, the wonderful wizard of Oz." Now let me tell you something. There are fifty-year-old French women who have never heard of Dorothy, or Toto, or the Tin Man, or the Scarecrow, or the Cowardly Lion.

I didn't even begin to try and explain.

Mona finds the unfamiliarity with this classic film equally perplexing, and then says she often has difficulty breathing, "I know I can walk, but I don't *really* think I can breathe." I remember Thây's breath meditation instructions from Day 20: "Breathing in, I know I am alive." Still, I am astounded by the Irish pilgrim's proclamation. I examine her pint-sized elfin body. "How can she manage to basically speed-walk *and* talk? She must be breathing."

With a mini powerhouse at my side, I remember the first time I experienced a mindful breath. It was through the practice of yoga, soon after the death of my mother. It was a seemingly simple task—I had been instructed to sit and observe the sound and sensation of each breath as it moved in and out of my body. I know what Mona is trying to communicate when she says that she can't *really* breathe. She is not aware of her breath. But here at the monastery, while being instructed to practice conscious breathing—concentrating on the sound and sensation of her breath—my new friend realized that there was a connection missing. Mona tells me now that she had been so cut off from her body during years of a medicated depression that awareness of her life force—her breath—had become incredibly weak. The petite Irishwoman's stride breaks slightly, enough time for me to notice the rows of brown sunflowers on dark furry stalks lining this country road, their jaundiced November petals curling in on cold, droopy heads.

Years ago, my early days of conscious breathing had been full of surprising discoveries. Paying attention to the fact that I was breathing unveiled what the yogis call a "latent power." Whenever I devotedly focused on my breath, I shifted from *thinking* into *feeling*. My mind rested, which then allowed my body to rest. I have heard many stories of difficult health issues being resolved from simple breath meditations, and I myself have felt physically stronger through these practices. Walking on this dirt road in France, a wave of gratitude washes over me. It seems miraculous that powerful and good change comes from such a simple thing as mindful breathing. I remind myself now that when the right kind of attention is paid to anything, there is a positive response. Things bloom when they are lovingly cared for. It is no surprise, then, that vitality and insight bloom from a conscious breath.

And now, as I clip along this country road, exactly two paces behind a woman who is half my size, I am thankful that my pixie-like speedy companion is also learning mindful breathing here at the monastery. The healing and transformative power inherent in a conscious breath is immense.

We have made it back to New Hamlet, but I feel more stressed than before the walk. Next time, I will walk with a nun. The pixie was too fast for me, and my heart continues to race. I don't want to suffer the many negative consequences of breathing without full awareness. This breath is a lifeline to that true Home within. The power of conscious breathing is not to be underestimated. Our breath will not last forever.

☞ Day 30 ☜

Catalysts:
Tsunamis, Wars, and
Burning Monks

The wax rose in the moth's body from her soaking abdo-
men to her thorax to the jagged hole where her head should
be, and widened into flame, a saffron-yellow flame that
robed her to the ground like any immolating monk.

—ANNIE DILLARD

On June 16, 1963, Buddhist monk Thich Quang Duc immolated himself in downtown Saigon. Many accounts say that Quang Duc set himself aflame to protest religious persecution against Buddhist monks under the Diem regime, and not the Vietnam War directly. However, Diem would not have been in power had it not been for U.S. intervention in Vietnam. Serenely sitting in flames, as if floating on a lotus leaf, this unusually valiant monk gave his life to create a transformation in people's consciousness during a brutal war and repressive political regime.

Thich Nhat Hanh's face changes as he speaks of his fellow monk today. I can't quite describe the alteration exactly, other than to say it's as if the monk is burning now. There is a long pause. You could hear a pin drop on the monastery floor. The immensity of this act of self-immolation hangs thick in the air.

Journalist David Halberstam was a witness to history: "A Buddhist monk sits still as stone, engulfed in flames. His body was slowly withering and shriveling up, his head blackening and charring. In the air the smell of burning flesh . . . I was too shocked to cry."

Thich Nhat Hanh deciphered the greater message in his fellow monk's self-immolation. "When Thich Quang Duc made himself into a human torch, people all over the world had to recognize that Vietnam was a land on fire, and they had to do something about it."

Before speaking of the brave monk's astonishing act, Thây opened his talk today by recalling the Asian tsunami of 2004, the numerous deaths it caused, and the message that lay in that disaster. For Thây, the tsunami deaths had been a catalyst that triggered his deep feelings of sadness for the many lives lost during the Vietnam War, in his homeland.

My ears immediately pricked up. Just a few days ago, I had recalled my time in India during the catastrophic tsunami while Thây had been teaching us the importance of awakening ourselves to the reality of suffering in the world. And now the Zen master was talking of the disaster directly.

On December 26, 2004, I was near the southern coastal city of Chennai, India, on day six of a ten-day Buddhist silent meditation retreat—absolutely no speaking for the duration of the course. When the big wave hit, the facilitators decided not to break the code of silence, which meant that none of the retreat participants were informed of the disaster. For four long days, my family back in Canada agonized over my safety. Telephone lines in India had jammed, with hundreds of worried people around the world attempting to get in touch with their loved ones. As a result, many families, including mine, could not get through.

On December 30, the meditation course finished, silence was lifted, and all the participants were finally told of the disaster. It had been a bizarre way to finish a retreat. I frantically tried to get through to Canada, but the phone lines were still jammed. Eventually I managed to convince an operator of the urgency of my call. Relieved to hear the voice of my eldest brother, David, I quickly burst into tears. My devoted brother had been about to board a plane to India in search of his only sister. That day, we had a conversation I'll never forget. As brothers and sisters we often take one another's love and support for granted, but during times of crisis, with the possibility that all may be forever changed, we snap out of our lazy affection. Instead, we voice our love for one another. During this cherished phone conversation, I had assured my brother of my safety and was overjoyed to feel his palpable relief, with this vast ocean between us.

"Like a lotus flower blossoming in a sea of fire, suffering is around you, but you retain your freedom."

Thich Nhat Hanh is comparing Thich Quang Duc's ability to remain serene, even as flames scorched his beautiful head, with our opportunity to bravely face the agony that surrounds us. To burn alive is to experience excruciating pain. And to have the capacity to bear that immense suffering with grace and composure is a strength that virtually none of us will ever have to summon. With this image seared in my mind, I feel courage ascend, and remember that bravery is elemental for taking refuge within the wise self.

Thây has a gentle but firm way of emphasizing vital information. Several times over the last month, in the most non-judgmental of ways, Thây has strongly advised us to *not exaggerate* our pain, as there is destruction in that amplification. The Buddhist teacher uses the metaphor of being struck by an arrow: Of course that first strike will cause some wound or pain. "But if, later on, a second arrow strikes that same wound, your suffering will increase tremendously. Your exaggeration is like the second arrow. A good practitioner doesn't let the second arrow come. The second arrow is your despair and anger toward the initial pain from the first strike." Thây stresses that if we let that second arrow strike, our pain may not only double, it could be ten times more intense; "Despair is a very powerful arrow."

I think about how often I have exaggerated various pains, and allowed those second sharp arrows to strike— those torturous mental thoughts and fears surrounding some injury. Thây suggests using the power of mindfulness to recognize *what is*. "Right Mindfulness accepts everything without judging or reacting."

I have often amplified what is and made it into what is not. Time to stop that.

Sometime after I returned home from the monastery, I put a photo on my refrigerator door of Thich Quang Duc as he sat quietly engulfed in flames in a Saigon intersection during the Vietnam War in 1963. This image of self-immolation reminds me of death, just like the bejeweled skeleton in the meditation hall. But mostly it inspires me to be courageous and to not waste time. The first friend I invited over for dinner after I had put the flaming monk on my fridge wasn't quite so open to its message. My friend was quite puzzled as to why I would *want* to look at this kind of image daily. I won't even describe the look on my brother Iain's face when he saw it.

Thich Quang Duc is my *memento mori*. He reminds me to live deeply in every moment, the only way to feel truly Home. All of us need this prompting. Our life goes by in a flash.

171

⌐ Day 31 ⌐

Expansion:
GET OUT OF YOUR SMALL SELF

An individual has not started living until he can rise above the narrow confines of his individualistic concerns to the broader concerns of all humanity.

—MARTIN LUTHER KING, JR.

Each nun of New Hamlet has her own meditation seat in the hall, and visitors choose from the remaining places. One morning, I asked a Sister why this is, and she replied that one builds a certain quality of vibration by sitting repeatedly in the same place, and that this was supportive and good for the Sisters. This perhaps explains why the lay practitioners intuitively gravitate toward the same place each time. Whether or not that is possible depends on when you arrive in the hall. I tend to be a last-minute sort, and so while I am not ever late, I am often arriving in the hall with just a few minutes to spare before the meditation begins. This means fewer open seats. The last seats are those that put your nose a few inches from a stone brick wall. I am in a nose-on-brick-wall seat today.

The bell chimes for the meditations to begin. The lead Sister opens with a chant, guiding us to "breathe in with the majestic mountain, and breathe out with the majestic mountain." I am not into the mountain today. My immediate neighbor loudly exhales. The rustling winter coat is in the hall. And then there's the drab grey, damp stone directly in front of my face. In the next moments, like a cacophony of out of tune instruments, a band of physical quirks rear their ugly heads, one by discordant one. My left eye twitches. My throat tightens. The back of my neck itches, and a heavy stone sits in the cavity that formerly held my heart. In less than three minutes I am consumed by physical discomfort, impatience, and mental fatigue.

I do not want to sit here with claustrophobia as my companion. I do not want to hear the whoosh of the parka every two minutes, or the exhausted exhales. I do not want to meditate today. I leave the hall two hours later, having not concentrated for one single moment.

"Sitting meditation is not for fighting. You must enjoy sitting." Thây says this a lot.

A nasty virus is making its insidious way through the halls of New Hamlet, and I have succumbed to its creeping attack. My feverish head is throbbing, knives are slicing my throat, and every single one of my muscles is leaden with a dull ache. Standing in the breakfast line, I now count at least ten other flu-ravaged beings. I am the eleventh sorry soul.

After a liquid breakfast, back up in my room alone, things worsen. The flu has somehow catapulted me into my despairing past. Memories of the comically ill-suited romantic companions of my recent history, short-lived relationships though they were, flood my mind. Even if I've now had the half-epiphany of recognizing that all of these incompatible men surfaced only after my father

173

died, perhaps explaining the psychology of my inane choices, the memories of, say, Alfred's complete absence of genuineness still baffles me. That one shifty eye, never more than half open, should have tipped me off to some sinister leanings. In this flu-ravaged moment of lament, the dreadful choices of my past surface for the dark memories that they are and I am in a gaping crevasse, unable to climb out.

With these gloomy thoughts I am exaggerating both my physical and mental pain. I am allowing the second arrow of aversion to strike me, right in my already dagger-stung raw throat. And all the while, the rumination cycle continues. I blow all of my problems way out of proportion, and then the only matter of concern to me is my own comfort and how to get it back. To make matters worse, once I realize this exaggeration and blatant self-centeredness, self-loathing joins the fun. I write this in my journal: "MARY GET OUT OF YOUR SMALL SELF."

When French scientist Blaise Pascal said, "All of man's problems come from his inability to sit quietly in a room alone," he was on to something.

Even though I can't seem to reign in my crazy mind today, my one consolation is that I am aware that I am amplifying my pain, even as I allow those bad feelings to inflate. Thây has pointed to a commonly veiled human tendency—this exaggeration of our various pains and problems. And now I see it clearly. But that second arrow has firmly sunken in, and I wonder if I will ever be able to unfailingly recognize my strength—to connect my mind and body in such a way as to live safely in the comfort of this calm inner Home no matter what tornado thunderously swirls about.

As I pay close attention to these miserable things that plague me, I feel worse. "It is much better to think of other people's well-being," I decide, "rather than shining a spotlight on my own vexing problems." I finally relax—a bit—but it takes some work to soften.

174

Thich Nhat Hanh teaches that we shouldn't spend too much time alone, as that solitude can feed this ruminating tendency. Fixating on personal issues is exhausting. I know that I am capable of expanding far beyond the narrow confines of me, so why don't I always do that? Why don't I think about other people in the world more often? Today, alone in my shoebox of a room in a monastery far from home, I finally remember that to feel emotionally balanced, not to mention useful, I've got to stop this improper focus on my concerns. I've just got to.

In protest against the repressive U.S.-backed regime in South Vietnam, more than thirty monks gave up their lives by setting their sacred bodies aflame. The online journal *Time Asia* reported that in 1965, after yet another Buddhist self-immolation, Thich Nhat Hanh wrote to the American civil rights leader Martin Luther King, Jr.: "The monks who burned themselves did not aim at the death of the oppressors, but only at a change in their policy. Their enemies are not man. They are intolerance, fanaticism, dictatorship, cupidity, hatred, and discrimination, which lie within the heart of man." Thich Nhat Hanh led King, and, by extension, the American public sentiment, to oppose the fighting in Vietnam.

Some weeks after I returned home from France, I read James Lovelock's *The Vanishing Face of Gaia.* Just like Thich Nhat Hanh, and every single one of the Buddhist monks who had burned their bodies to bring forth freedom for the Vietnamese, Lovelock knows the importance of expanding one's thinking beyond the small self. Lovelock is a crusading ninety-two-year-old independent scientist, and the originator of the Gaia Theory, a proposal that the earth, ecosystems, and the totality of life is a self-regulating evolving system with the goal of encouraging life. Lovelock recognizes that "above all, humans hate any conspicuous change in their daily way of life and view of the future." And even though Lovelock was pointing to the constricting selfishness that prevents us from changing indulgent habits that destroy the environment, I viewed those same ecology-destroying habits—the ones that people *think* increase their happiness—as the very routines that actually limit happiness levels. I'm much happier biking than driving a car, for example. But there have been many occasions when I have felt the narrow confines of my limiting small self, and my attachment to joy-busting habits. I have also experienced glimmers of expansion and selflessness. I want to multiply those glimmers.

In those same weeks after my sojourn, I did understand more clearly that individual concerns must not eclipse the broader reality for millions of people. That insight came partly because of the communal living arrangement at the monastery. It had been the kind of environment that caused me to call greater attention to the importance of considering not only all the many different people sharing life on the monastery grounds, but also the conditions in which millions of people live around the world.

⁓⊗⊙⊗⁓

In *The Heart of the Buddha's Teachings*, Thich Nhat Hanh defines *prajna paramita* as "the highest kind of understanding, free from all knowledge, concepts, ideas, and views." We gain this insight from being present, mindful, and concentrated in our lives. Thây sheds light on the utility of this practice:

> The suffering inside of you reflects the suffering of the world. That's why you have to

remove your own suffering in order to help
the world. When you have understood your
own suffering, you can understand the others' suffering. Then, when you look at them,
you look at them differently—you understand their suffering. You look at them with
the eyes of compassion. When the other sees
you look at them with compassion, immediately they will suffer less.

I have a genuine moment of hoping that Alfred's
wonky eye is better.

And there it is. One does need to focus on one's
internal pain, but in the proper way, so as to identify it,
accept it, and then do something productive to alleviate
it. Usually, self-pity and that second destructive arrow of
exaggeration sneak in. Again, if we let that second arrow
insidiously jab away at us, we will only suffer more. Wal-
lowing in our own horrible muck, we are absolutely use-
less to the world.

The right kind of attention toward one's own suffering is the key to liberating ourselves from despair. Free
from despondency, we connect with the power of our
enduring strength. Only then can we serve humanity.

☞ Day 32 ☜

Interdependence:
No Shit, No Flower

Contemplation is the keen awareness of the interdependence of all things.

—THOMAS MERTON

Tormented by my afflictions in the chilly meditation hall this morning, I try to see the happiness somewhere in the depths of my dis-ease. Thây tells me it is there. I close my eyes. My breath is feeble, but it's there. I take the elevator down into my body. Descending out of my thinking mind brings some relief, even if it's mild. My breathing becomes a little less weak. My mind and body start communicating because I am attending to my breath. And even though my shoulders are like cement blocks, the dull pain doesn't distress me in the same way. My relationship toward my sickly body becomes a little more balanced—I'm not fighting the reality of what is there. This neutral state then allows me to listen more carefully to the Zen master now speaking, "Just as a beautiful lotus flower blossoms out of mud, happiness can blossom from suffering." In fact, our suffering is *essential* for our happiness. Yes, he said "essential." And then even while I wished it wasn't so, he said this: "Happiness is made up of non-happiness elements." We can't know happiness without knowing suffering.

When Thây had first used the lotus image to demonstrate the freedom that Thich Quang Duc had been capable of—his wholly remarkable calm, even while flames licked his serene body in that Vietnam square— the Zen master was helping us see that the brave monk's liberation is available to all of us, no matter what kind of fiery agony is there. Today, I am asked to look deeper still. Not only does the lotus flower represent freedom, but it also symbolizes our joy—the happiness that would not exist without the surrounding chaotic mud—our various problems. The mud is necessary. The mud creates the flower, is responsible for the joy. The two are dependent on each other. Thây points out, "A good gardener knows the way to turn mud into compost so that beautiful flowers can grow." The trick, I think now, is to somehow appreciate the muck that appears in life as nourishing compost for some insight-filled future joy, and not just view it as woeful muck. Only then will it be possible to cultivate joy. If I am not able to transform the muck into compost—if I am a lousy gardener—I will only see the muck as joy-busting muck.

"You cannot grow a lotus flower on a marble surface."

When Thây said this just now, I understood it as anyone would—truths are obvious once revealed, especially with a beautiful metaphor. I am reminded of the times I haven't been able to cultivate joy if conditions aren't just right. But I once had a great boyfriend who could. Doug absolutely loved canoeing on remote rivers, as I did. However, sometimes there were big stretches of land between these rivers, which required portaging— strapping all of your camping gear on your back, lifting

179

up a heavy canoe, and trekking through mosquito-ridden forests in the blazing summer heat. Doug loved it. I hated it. The pioneer seemed to relish the hard labor. I didn't know it at the time, but Doug had a deep understanding of the inter-being of pain and joy. I see that now. My wise friend knew that the irritation of dragging a cumbersome canoe through bug-ridden bushes was contingent on actualizing great joy on the open river. The two could not exist without each other. I just wanted to get to the river, whereas Doug accepted and embraced both the painful path leading to the river and the river itself.

<hr/>

I am definitely grumpy and sick, but somehow Thây's words melt into me. Good things can and do come from challenges, difficulties and pain, in fact hardship is essential to growth. Thây has a beautiful way of explaining this. If we can look deeply into our suffering with the right view, we will accept, and then begin to understand the nature or root of that pain. Understanding our suffering then gives rise to compassion and love within. Understanding, compassion and love are the very foundation of happiness. Thây points out that, "A person who has no compassion or love within themselves can never relate to another human being." The ability to relate to others is, of course, essential for happiness. Thây advises us to not discriminate against our suffering. We simply need to "make good use of the suffering, the mud, in order to nourish the flower of happiness." Free from anger, fear and despair toward that pain, we become very lucid. Lucidity has the power to give us great insight to help ourselves. When we take care of ourselves properly, only then can we be of some benefit to others.

Here in the Dharma Hall, the intricacies of this truth are revealed in a metaphorically beautiful way.

And in a manner that will stay with me. I feel this now. This teaching will be retained within my mind because of the delicate strength of the lotus image. An exquisite, pristine, white lotus bloom fills my mind now. As I breathe, the flower opens and breathes with me. My skin transforms into the softness of the petals, and the flower becomes my body. Blooming. Breathing. Blooming. Repose comes. Gentleness glides through my body, caressing the discomfort, tenderly embracing my wounds. I breathe. The white lotus breathes. I bloom. The white lotus blooms. Breathing. Blooming. Breathing. A radiant joy is within me. It is the brilliant white lotus flower. It was there all along.

<hr />

The lotus flower is such a masterful image—fragrant flowers and smelly muck inter-are, to use Thây's idiom. In fact, it is impossible to have one without the other—no shit, no flower. The Zen Buddhist continues teaching: "Happiness and suffering inter-are. Like two sides of a coin, one cannot exist without the other. But to be able to truly see the lotus in the mud—the joy in the suffering, you must be able to look very deeply. This is called the *non-dualistic look*—seeing the oneness in all phenomena."

The monk lifts up his left hand and then his right and says, "It is true that where there is left, its opposite, right, also exists." Then Thây says this great thing: "If politically you are on the left, do not wish for the right to disappear altogether." Without the right, there can be no left. How true.

Buddhists call this world of ours the "historical dimension." In *no death, no fear*, Thây elaborates: "We look upon reality in our daily lives through the historical dimension, but we can also look upon the same reality in the ultimate dimension." If I look deep into ugliness, for example, I will see its opposite, beauty, and I will be touching the ultimate dimension where that narrow, dualistic way of looking at things is transcended.

Thây emphasizes that of course all of us must take care of our daily or historical concerns—unfortunately, we all have to do our taxes, and make our beds—but we also need to address our ultimate concerns. In *no death, no fear*, Thich Nhat Hanh continues: "When we look for God or nirvana or the deepest kind of peace, we are concerned about the ultimate. We are not only concerned with the facts of daily life—fame, profit, or our position in society and our projects—but we are also concerned about our true nature. To meditate deeply is to begin to fulfill our ultimate concern."

In the Dharma talk today, Thây emphasizes that "In order to go beyond, you must accept the impermanence of all things in our world." Nothing lasts forever here on earth. This is an essential understanding of a liberated mind. By contemplating the impermanent nature of everything, we realize that our pain is not endless—a vital understanding for our mental health and well-being.

When Thây pointed directly to the truth of impermanence by saying, "Our suffering is impermanent just like everything else," the collective relief I felt in this hall of silent pilgrims, monks, and nuns was immense.

And not only is it good to know that suffering can't possibly last, but there is something about anguish that encourages useful introspection. That deep looking generates insight. And joy lives in that wisdom. Then, we finally taste freedom. Aeschylus, the Greek father of tragedy, may have been right when he said, "Man must suffer to be wise."

After lunch today, I see the Willem Dafoe lookalike monk. He likes his coffee. He is sitting, gracefully, like a monk sits, at a table in the dining hall with his own

French press, sipping away. Espresso vapors fill the air. The American monk tells me that before being ordained by Thich Nhat Hanh, only one year ago, he lived off coffee. Now he drinks far less of it. I sit down across from this caffeine-loving Brother, secretly delighted to know that some monks drink this stimulating brew. Our conversation turns to yoga. The Willem Dafoe looka-like asks if I can suggest some suitable exercises. Of course I can. After all, I have been regularly teaching the nuns a series of ancient Buddhist yoga techniques called The Five Tibetans. Many cold November mornings I stand happily with eight smiling, shiny baldheads in the meditation hall and instruct this group of devoted Sisters to *"Inspirer par le nez, et expirer par le bouche."* In a Buddhist monastery, with Vietnamese nuns, I demonstrate sacred techniques from India in the beautiful language of French.

Because it is not permitted for monks and nuns or monks and women to be alone together, I am not allowed to teach these Tibetan Buddhist techniques to the Brother I am so very fond of. I tell the yoga-loving monk that I will write some instructions for him. We smile. I think again of the monk's choice to become celibate, and wonder if all the monks and nuns here keep that vow. I sense that this genial monk does. Something about the way he doesn't avoid looking at me. It is said that the Buddha, while sitting under the Boddhi tree the night of his enlightenment, experienced visions of seductresses. These dangerously enticing women attempted to break the Buddha's discipline. Not only was the Buddha steadfast, but he could easily look the sirens in the eye with neither grasping nor aversion. I've noticed some of the monks here don't even glance at women, let alone befriend them, like the Willem Dafoe lookalike monk has done with me. I suppose for some, it is wise to avoid looking altogether. I am glad, though, that this very Buddha-like Buddhist monk can easily look me straight in the eye.

One of the things that Thây said today was that we make the mistake of thinking that we have to remove 100 percent of our suffering in order to be happy—that is just not true, or even possible. We can have some happiness amidst our own particular type of pain. Each of us has some amount of suffering. The trick, the Zen teacher says, is to think to yourself, "Let me handle this pain with dignity." Thây again emphasized, as he did on the first day of my sojourn, that it would be an injustice to the Buddha to infer that the enlightened being meant that all is suffering (as some people interpret the First Noble Truth to mean). This is not true. Thich Nhat Hanh then firmly said, "Life is suffering? No. Life is happiness? No. Both exist at the same time." We must relate to both the unhappy elements and the happy elements in our lives with the right view. Our task is to transform the suffering that exists—to have a new relationship with it so that it does not destroy us.

Our troubled times are launching pads from which we can leap into wisdom-filled, mature happiness. If it weren't for the deaths of my parents, I wouldn't be on this pilgrimage now—this wisdom-filled journey. If it weren't for the mud of my pain, I wouldn't be able to grow the lotuses of joy that are in me now.

Everything depends on everything else. We simply need to understand how to work with all that appears in our life.

❧ Day 33 ❧

Transcendence:
The Angel Who Came to Me

The darkest hour is just before dawn.

—ENGLISH PROVERB

Death would be easier. Today my nasty flu is a hundred times worse, and I have yet another chance to identify the truth that my suffering and happiness coexist. Even though it's up to me whether or not I turn the muck of this sickness into the compost that will nourish joy, it would be much more pleasant to just feel well.

I am so sick that I skip everything today—the morning meditations, a taped Dharma talk in the hall, walking meditation, my work duties, and all the meals. I stay in my room all day. Taking refuge in myself, no matter what is happening, seems impossible. I just don't see how I can do it when I feel so awful.

Arrows are flying into me from all over the place.

But I know that this is my big chance. If I can somehow look deep into my pain—even this miniscule and relatively insignificant type of suffering—there will be some

185

delight under there. I must remember that this discomfort is the door to some deeper understanding and liveliness. It is toughening me up. If I can relate properly to this illness within, some insight will come. But at the moment, it seems impossible to dive deep into this pain—I'd rather avoid it. I end up feeling sorry for myself again. By late afternoon, I am too sick and troubled to sleep, so I wearily wander down to the kitchen to refill my thermos with hot ginger tea. Once there, I see some of my friends milling about, and pause to talk with three of them.

As I listen to my spiritual comrades relay their varying activities from the day, a gentle, warm touch—soft as a butterfly—lights on my shoulder. I turn round to find myself peering into the eyes of an angel. The angelic being is in the form of a lithe Vietnamese nun, with a swan-like neck and radiant glow. It turns out that this benevolent Sister had heard I was unwell and came looking for me. She now takes both my hands in hers, and with a velvet voice says, "Let me give you a healing massage." Sweeter words I have never heard. Unsurprisingly, I immediately feel delight. The angel/nun takes my hand in hers and leads me up to my room.

The nun's hand is the hand of the Buddha.

The angel/nun asks me to lie on my stomach. I gratefully sink into the monastic cot that now has the feeling of a cushy king sized bed. The angel's delicate hand gently lifts my shirt. My muscles soften with joyous expectancy, and my breath becomes light and fluid. I am in such a state of thankfulness that I am not even aware of my horrendous afflictions. I smell some kind of Chinese ointment that I recognize as tiger balm, and the angel begins applying the healing cream on my back with some kind of object. I realize later that she had used the back of a ceramic spoon in sweeping lines along my muscles, exactly where they hurt so much.

186

I flutter one eyelid open to see that everything in the room emits a warm golden glow. And there is an angel floating over me.

Now, I've had some great massages in my life, but I have never felt the way I do now. I will try to explain. The angel/nun is deeply immersed in the act of massaging me. Her hands touch me from the goodness of her heart. She simply wants to help me feel better. And who am I? This Sister is not one of the nuns I have become good friends with here. Before today, I had seen her around, but just at a distance. The love I feel coming from her now almost causes me to burst into tears. Instead of crying, though, I become deeply relaxed, thankful, and full of joy. This is it. The epiphany is immediate. This is what Thây means when he says, "There is a lotus in the mud. There is joy in suffering." I finally get it.

Then for a split second my mind wanders, and I think, "I wonder how long the angel will massage me. It feels *sooo* good. I hope it will continue for a long time." And in those few moments of wondering, I disconnect from the glorious feeling. My craving has temporarily obliterated my joy.

I once heard the Buddhist scholar Robert Thurman talk about how we are never really satisfied. "When we are in an unpleasant state, all we can think of is, When will it be over? Similarly, when we are experiencing pleasant sensations, we are in danger of thinking, When will the good time be over? The good time is over the instant we think that."

The sacred back rub finishes and I dreamily open my eyes. Radiant light surrounds the blessed nun. She is pressing her hands together at her heart and bowing her luminous face, on that impossibly long neck, over my deeply relaxed body. I now know the true definition of beatific. I press my hands together and bow to my angelic Sister.

I remember hearing Thây say that whenever you feel unable to do something, ask the Buddha to come and take your hand, and then you will have strength. The Buddha will be doing that thing for you—whatever you need him to do. Upon returning home from my pilgrimage, this advice stuck with me.

After I left Plum Village, while in Bordeaux, I was revisited by this terrible flu bug that now assaults my every cell. It hitched a ride with me all the way home to Toronto. My transatlantic flight had been horrific, and I had arrived home to a freezing Canadian winter, at midnight, my illness and fatigue much worse. At that time, I had no family around, as my brother Iain was out of town, and the rest of my family live outside of Toronto. I was to stay temporarily in Iain's condo, and upon arriving there I immediately crawled into bed, but I couldn't sleep. There was no food or drink in the condo and my sickness was increasing from lack of nutrition. But I couldn't very well call a friend at 1:00 a.m. to bring me some orange juice.

Lying in bed that night, I remembered both Thây's teaching and the angelic nun from this day. On that dark somber night, I closed my eyes and visualized the Buddha floating down to me, descending from some glorious and golden nirvana. I felt the Buddha take my hand. The Buddha helped me get up, wrapped a scarf around my head, and put my coat on me. Holding my limp hand, the Buddha led me out the door, down the elevator, and into the corner store. We bought orange juice. Then we promptly turned around, went back into the building, up the elevator, and into the condo. Two big glasses of orange juice later, the enlightened one tucked me into bed and I slept like a baby through the night.

Sometimes I am so mired in my own discomfort that I shine a burning spotlight on that pain. That wrong kind of attention just makes the suffering worse. My ferocious ailment in the monastery led to the most transcendent massage of my life. And my sickness back in Canada compelled me to call on the Buddha's strength. In both cases, the mud of my sickness became compost for the glorious white lotus flower—my rapturous delight and healing. Thich Nhat Hanh has shown me that the power to turn poison into medicine is available to all of us. Bitter pain can either kill or become a potion for wisdom and bliss. The choice is ours.

Non-Self:
The Damning of the Ego

What we have done for ourselves alone, dies with us;
what we have done for others and the world remains and
is immortal.

—ALBERT PIKE

"Damn ego. What is this extreme attachment to satisfying my own self? Why do I cherish this self so
much? What's the point of having an ego in the first
place—the universe's cruel joke? This self-centeredness
is the cause of so much of my suffering. . . ." Blah, blah,
blah, goes my mind. Thây is certainly right about one
thing—the ocean of life is definitely stormy.

I am grumpy because I am still sick. The joy I felt
yesterday during that sacred massage from the angel
has vanished into thin air. One of my favorite Sisters,
while equally flu-struck, has continued her duties around
the monastery, obviously graced with the steadiest of
minds. She has not missed any of Thây's Dharma talks,
and I haven't heard a peep from her in the form of any

complaint. I suppose her resilience is built in to her very fiber. Still, when I see her today, and commend her strength, she doesn't think it's anything out of the ordinary, or especially unique.

This Sister does not allow any second arrow to escalate the pain of any wound.

"Often we can be in our own country but still not feel that we are *Home*." Thây uttered this piece of wisdom earlier today. Sick or not, I feel exactly the same kind of "homelessness" here, in France, that I experience in my own country. I left my geographical home in search of an abiding steadiness that I wasn't sure I could find there. But it's Day 34 of the retreat, and I am unstable and shaky, as if I'm crossing a suspension bridge in high winds. Halfway around the world and yet I have the exact same torturous thoughts here that invade my mind there. Yes, being physically unwell is exacerbating the insecurity, and yes, I know there is a path through—the fortress is within sight—but I really need to get a grip and reign in my unruly mind.

Earlier today, Thich Nhat Hanh talked of Jesus. I love a Buddhist monk who freely refers to a Christian prophet. Thây pointed out that Jesus was looking for his true Home and that the desolate state of loneliness had induced a seeking within this redeemer of man. As we all know, ultimately, Jesus did find this wise refuge, and then went on to selflessly guide others toward their own true Home through His insightful teachings.

To realize Home no matter where I am—how brilliant would that be? I have cast myself out of my home in order to find my Home.

The sage monk here is doing just what Jesus is said to have shepherded centuries ago. He is guiding me toward my true Home—the one that is not a geographical place. The Buddhist monk is at the helm, navigating my journey through the maze that is my life. I am being led in the direction that will decrease my selfishness, open compassion, and lessen my suffering. I am being encouraged to connect my mind and body through mindfulness so that it will be natural for me to think of others, to be generous and kind. These guideposts are all around me here. I see the monastic's careful attention toward others. I reflect on absolutely everything within these monastery walls. There is nothing else to do. In Toronto I readily distract myself with a typical triad of friends, films, and food. There are friends and food here too, but the quality of the communing is different. In Plum Village, the backdrop of the sacred is ever present.

I have not yet mastered the Buddhist art of suffering, of having the proper kind of attention toward my pain. I am exaggerating my discomfort again today. Did I mention that my sickness stubbornly persists? That "taking refuge in yourself" thing seems as inaccessible as a locked door with no key.

Thây again points directly to truth: "We worry about our own future, but we fail to worry about the future of the other because we think that our happiness has nothing to do with the happiness of the other. This idea of 'self' and 'other' gives rise to immeasurable suffering."

Understanding the essential Buddhist teaching of non-self reduces self-absorbtion, and therefore we become happier. I discovered this liberating teaching of the Buddha through Thây early in my journey. The Buddhist scholar distilled this teaching down to its pure meaning: "What we call a self is made only of non-self elements." Again, in simple terms, when I look deep within myself, I see the cosmos. What I think of as "me" is simply a bunch of "non-me" things coming together to make "me." Without all of these "non-human" elements, like sunshine, earth, minerals, water, my education, the apple I am now eating, and so on, I cannot exist. So what is my "self," then? This bundle of muscles and nerves and blood and bones that I think of as me is just that—masses of cells that wouldn't exist without, say, the oatmeal I ate this morning, or my mother, or the sun, or bacteria, or rain. My very existence comes from things that are not me. Thich Nhat Hanh has helped me to see this very clearly.

Thây reveals that "the teachings of impermanence and non-self were offered by the Buddha as keys to unlock the door of reality." If I can remember that nothing lasts forever, then I will have an easier time accepting the truth of non-self, that everything is simply made up of things it is not.

On that pivotal day halfway through my journey, Taka and her violin taught me about impermanence. In those moments, as the melancholic woman brought to life her masterful rendition of Bach, I felt the musical notes appear and disappear. I felt highly aware of the constantly changing nature of those sacred sounds. And that insight opened me up to the reality that absolutely everything in existence is constantly changing. Each vibratory note that was plucked on that violin came and went.

Things cannot remain the same for two consecutive moments. Therefore, how could I remain the same? Everything about me is in constant flux. My emotions, my body weight, my thoughts, the length of my fingernails, the wrinkles around my eyes—all are changing as I write this. Therefore, my permanent self in one particular kind of form cannot possibly exist. And thus I can more easily comprehend non-self. What is this me? Like the violin, the music coming from it, and the violinist herself, I can't possibly be the exact same *being* from moment to moment—in time or in space. This is a comforting thought while I feel so awfully sick. I know my illness won't last forever. And not only that, but if I can look deeply enough into impermanence and non-self, I will touch *nirvana*—the Buddhist term for the complete silencing of all concepts, a heavenly abode. Pure freedom. To be the sovereign of my mind would be like unearthing the riches of a gold mine. The gift of liberation is definitely worth digging for.

Earlier in the week, one of the pilgrims had organized a cookie baking crew with several of the women here at New Hamlet. Somehow I hadn't heard about it. The afternoon of the cookie baking, I had come down from my room to the kitchen for a cup of tea, only to smell the delicious aroma of freshly baked cinnamon sugar. Dollops of fresh cookie dough in tiny mountains sat on six-foot-long trays, while several other pans perched by windows displayed gloriously warm, brown baked treats. There were cookies everywhere, and the bakers were eating them.

Now, let me just say that cookies are a very special treat when one is living the life of a monastic. I felt a bit sheepish about directly asking for a yummy morsel, however, as I hadn't helped bake them. And they were meant for an upcoming lay-friend's gathering. So, instead, I said everything else I could think of that might possibly persuade the cookie master to grace me with a rare and precious cinnamon-dusted biscuit. I complimented the team on their cookie-making skills. I told them they were kind. I even showed authentic dismay at somehow not hearing about the baking marathon, and said that if I'd known, I would've been the first to volunteer. Nothing worked.

I like the head baker—she is a lovely and kind Dutch woman. "What's going on?" I thought. "She's a nice person. Why isn't she offering me a cookie?" Discouraged and cookie-less, I hung my little head and crept away.

It is rather funny that this cookie incident happened to me, because in his books and Dharma talks, Thây has used the example of cookies to illuminate the teaching of non-self. Thich Nhat Hanh describes how in order to make cookies we need a bunch of "non-cookie" elements—the flour, sugar, butter, etc. . . . Then, when we bring all these cookie ingredients together as one, we have created something different than the individual items on their own. We have made cookie batter from things that are not cookie batter. And then, to bake the cookies, this batter that had previously been altogether as one, is separated on a tray. It is a great image. All of the baked cookies end up slightly different from each other in size and shape. Thây humorously suggests that should one cookie think itself better than another cookie because of its unique shape or color, that would be too bad. But we humans often do this—we very quickly and easily discriminate against our fellow human beings, our fellow baked cookies. We forget that in essence all of us are one, but simply operating in different shapes, sizes, and colors—different cookies, from the same batter.

Back in my room, disappointed at being snubbed by the cookie master, I remember something else. This head baker regularly attends the complimentary yoga classes I have been leading here at the monastery. Upon recalling this, I feel a little sad. Has she forgotten maybe? Or not connected the two? I reflect and realize that sometimes I also do this in life. I miss connections. There have been times when I have forgotten that grace comes from all directions, and so one should just be generous as much as possible.

This evening I am in bed reading The Diamond Sutra, from Thich Nhat Hanh's *The Diamond That Cuts Through Illusion*, which also happens to be the Willem Dafoe look-alike monk's current subject of study:

> We put a lot of energy into advancing technology in order to serve our lives better, and we exploit the non-human elements, such as the forests, rivers, and oceans, in order to do so. But, as we pollute and destroy nature, we pollute and destroy ourselves as well. The results of discriminating between human and non-human are global warming, pollution,

195

and the emergence of many strange diseases. In order to protect ourselves, we must protect the non-human elements. This fundamental understanding is needed if we want to protect our planet and ourselves.

As I close the book that cuts through illusion, my sickness drops away.

⌒ Day 35 ⌒

Space:
The Day I Looked Between the
Tree Branches

To me every hour of the light and dark is a miracle,
Every cubic inch of space is a miracle,
Every square yard of the surface of the earth is spread
with the same,
Every foot of the interior swarms with the same.
— WALT WHITMAN, "MIRACLES"

It's a crisp winter day and I am walking amongst the plum trees in the garden of New Hamlet. The grey, bare tree branches appear the same as they have for thirty-four days. But then I stop walking and gaze at one tree. My eyes switch focus to the open spaces between these tree arms that not long ago had been heavy with fruit and leaves. I shift my attention back and forth between the tree branches themselves and the rich space surrounding them. I do this several times. I close my eyes. There is only clarity. The space

197

holds me. I am contained by the space. I am experiencing the *space* rather than the *matter* within the space. Space surrounds me, and space is also within me.

> *Form is emptiness, emptiness is form.*
> —FROM *THE HEART OF UNDERSTANDING*
> BY *THICH NHAT HANH*

I think again of the two glasses that Thây had used to help us understand the Buddha's teaching on emptiness—one glass has tea in it, and a second glass has no tea. The second glass is empty of tea but it is not empty of air. I remind myself that to be empty or not empty, the glass has to be there. Emptiness does not mean non-existence. The emptiness of the glass does not mean the non-existence of the glass. The glass is there, but it is empty. I am here, but I am empty. "Empty of what?" I feel what Thây knows: "I am empty of a separate existence." I am made up of the cosmos and linked to everything within it. I am space and space is me.

The Willem Dafoe look-alike monk is across the grassy field, his familiar monastic head standing out amongst the others. I make my way over to him and say hello. As usual, we have the same easy, satisfying presence together. I ask the monk how he is doing. It turns out my favorite Brother had been unwell with a nasty flu bug, just like me. We are both feeling somewhat better today. I ask if I can take a photo of him. He says yes. I say that I will give him a copy for his family. With no discernible emotion, the Buddhist monk says that his father doesn't like to see him with a shaved head. We walk across the garden toward the bamboo forest. The monk stands in front of the thick foliage and it frames his bald monastic head distinctively. Jade green is the perfect backdrop for earth-toned robes. The monk seems happy and content. Why can't his father see what I see?

Here at Plum Village, the monastics call each other "my Brother" or "my Sister." If they want to distinguish between a monastic and a biological brother or sister, they will say, "my blood brother" or "my blood sister." After returning home, when I received an email from Sister Pine with the salutation, "Dear sister Mary," I was deeply moved, as I am neither her blood sister nor her monastic Sister. My Brother now says that we must take the photo quickly, as he must soon leave to pick up some visitors from the train station. This is his regular task.

The monk with the PhD in electrical engineering doubles as a chauffer. I wonder if he is slightly bored with this task of driving, and ask him if he misses the stimulation of his previous work back in the real world. My Brother tells me that he can spend a whole week reading just one Buddhist sutra over and over. This week he is reviewing the Diamond Sutra, the regular study and practice of which is said to help one cut through afflictions, ignorance, delusion, and illusion. I pause for a moment. The esoteric teachings of the Buddha are brilliant. Of course this devoted practitioner would have loads of stimulation for his mind. I watch the monk with the PhD walk away. He's off to the train station to collect more pilgrims.

Alone again, my company the sacred trees, I watch their woody branches move lightly in the gentle wind. It seems as if the expanse of the space is calling out to me. "There are lessons within the spaces between the lines of sacred sutras, too," I think, "just like in between the branches of these trees." I remember some lines from the teachings of Taoism: "We hammer wood for a house, but it is the inner space that makes it livable." I look down to the buildings of New Hamlet from the hill where I stand. They are beautifully built old stone farmhouses, transformed into reverent temples of the Buddha, and homes for his practitioners. "The space inside those buildings transforms people," I realize. The space inside is where all the good stuff happens. I think of two more lines from the Tao: "We work with being, but non-being is what we use." Another shift happens.

⁓⁓⁓

We are all held by the space, but it is not at the front of our consciousness. Many sages and saints have compared this quiet, open, vast space of ours to a "womb of creation." This space contains intelligence—it *is* an intelligence. I take a deep, full breath in and open my face into the blue above. The next instant, my head lowers and I bow. Again, I lift my eyes above the trees and into the azure sky. My exhale carries my head down, and my hands touch the dampness of the earth. In comes the next breath, and I ascend. The space around me seems thick and rich—it has always been thick and rich—but now I feel it. The next exhale drives the truth in deeper. A wise whisper is reminding me to be reverent of the nature that surrounds me.

And like this I continue to rise up and bow, rise up and bow, rise up and bow. Everything else falls away except my connection to the space. I swing my arms through the air and my freedom stretches with my limbs. There is wisdom within this space. I have taken refuge both within my self and within the space. What is within me is the same as what is outside of me. Taking refuge within equals taking refuge in the universal, open space. I see that clearly now. I have nothing to worry about. I let go and align myself with the intelligence of the space.

"The one who bows, and the one who is bowed to, are both, by their nature, empty."

When Thây said this earlier today, he was explaining that unless one has the actual experience of emptiness—and not simply the intellectual understanding or even acceptance of emptiness—then no communication is possible. The Zen teacher emphasized that true communication is possible between you and the Buddha, or between you and the tree, or between you and anyone or anything, only when you know that both you and the other are made up solely of things that you are not.

What is a tree? It is water, bark, leaves, roots, time, the sunshine, the minerals of the earth, the seed from which it grew, the gardener's hands that tilled the earth, and so on. So, what is a tree? It is simply a mass of things that it is not.

I remind myself again that, like the tree, I am simply made up of non-me things,. Therefore, I am empty of a separate self, but full of the whole universe, just as the Buddha is empty of a separate self but full of the whole universe. And you are empty of a separate self but full of the whole universe. All of us are deeply connected.

I take another bow.

When you understand non-self, you transcend the complexes of superiority, inferiority, and even equality. And then, only then, can you communicate with—bow to—the tree or the Buddha, or anyone or anything. Thich Nhat Hanh emphasizes that before this realization, it is not possible to truly bow to the Buddha. He said, "If you think the Buddha is something outside of yourself, you are mistaken. *To be* means to *inter-be* with everything."

Usually I am so stupidly attached to my body, my thoughts, and my excruciating emotions that I am not communicating with or paying attention to the wise expanse of the space both within me and surrounding me. My life cannot be contained in a small box, but sometimes I act as if it could be.

I am still standing at the top of the grassy hill on the grounds of New Hamlet, amongst my teachers, the plum tree branches. I don't know how long I have been bowing, but the sky has gone dark. As I walk down the hill, I remember something that Thây told us yesterday. In Vietnam people call their spouses *Nha toi*, which means "my Home." "In Vietnam, when someone walks up to your house looking for your wife, what they are really asking is this: 'Is your Home, home?' And if she is there, you can happily say, 'Yes, my Home is home.'" Thây said that all of us have this deep desire to have a Home, and we are lucky if we can find it, not only with a partner, but also with a spiritual practice and a community.

We spend our whole lives looking for our Home, but it is right here—in the Buddha (the wise ancient prophet), the Dharma (the spiritual teachings), and the Sangha (the community of like-minded people we surround ourselves with). These three places are our Homes. Thich Nhat Hanh reminded us that mindful breathing puts us in touch with these three refuges. He gracefully uttered these words: "Because your breath is part of you, you can touch yourself on your in-breath. Many of us don't know where our own self is. The in-breath gets you in touch with your cells where your roots are. Then you will be filled with your true Home."

My breath is leading me Home.

⌐ Day 36 ⌐

Transformation:
An Eighty-Four-Year-Old Monk
Becomes a Five-Year-Old Child

If the doors of perception were cleansed,
Everything would appear to man as it is, infinite.
—WILLIAM BLAKE,
THE MARRIAGE OF HEAVEN AND HELL

I t is late morning, the sky is pale blue and I am walking. Nearby, two smiling nuns are strolling hand in hand. Pure affection floats in the breeze. The Buddhist Sisters are moving as if they are one *being*.

I am mindful . . . of the plum trees, sleeping grapevines, tawny sunflowers on the cusp of transformation, and the loving Sisters walking through all of it. Everything is living and dying and being reborn, all at once. I carefully put one foot on the damp earth. A golden brown leaf lies rumpled at the front of my boot. Soon, the dead leaf will become the earth, and it will feed the same tree that it once hung from, this tree in front of me here. And after some time, another bud will sprout from the tree, and that bud will become another leaf. The leaf is in the leaf.

Today, I am "putting my mind in the sole of my foot," as Thây counsels.

Thây is leading the mindfulness walk today. His presence has sharpened my focus. After walking for some time, Thây pauses, causing everyone else to follow suit. A mix of around two hundred monks, nuns, men, women, and a few children now surround a tranquil pond of white lotuses, their roots hidden within the mud that is so essential for their beauty. Each of the four Hamlets of Plum Village has a sacred lotus pond as a reminder of the inter-being of suffering and joy—the necessity of painful muck in the creation of happiness. Because we have encircled the pond, I have a clear view of Thây, even though I am far from the front. In two distinct movements, the monk directs his gaze toward me, and then waves. I have never seen Thich Nhat Hanh wave before, let alone during a mindfulness walk. And with his hand in the air, the mystical being transforms into a five-year-old child. In one magical time-bending moment, Thây is not an eighty-four-year-old monk. His face is unquestionably that of a cherubic youth. I see deep into Thây's ageless soul. In the next instant, I instinctively mirror his motion back toward him, and as I wave, I too become my pristine, five-year-old self. The monk and me are two five-year-old beings together beyond time. It all happens in a few seconds.

Perhaps this shift in my consciousness is happening simply because I have been on this journey for thirty-six days, in the midst of wide-open vineyards, rolling hills, and fields that sprout gigantic tawny sunflowers in the summertime. Nature and its rhythms are rousing me from sleep. Or perhaps it's because earlier today, Thich Nhat Hanh said, "When you walk on the mother earth you must walk with reverence. You are walking on your mother." Or maybe it's due to my heightened sensitivity, spurred on by days of quiet contemplation with my Brothers and Sisters. Whatever the cause, the happy child within me—the innocent one who loves life—is here now.

In, out
Deep, slow
Calm, ease
Smile, release
Present moment, wonderful moment

Thich Nhat Hanh suggests silently repeating this poem of his during walking meditation, to enhance the healing power of mindful walking. I try this now, while walking near the delightfully happy entwined Sisters. I concentrate on the fact that I am breathing as I breathe in, and mentally vibrate the word "in." Simultaneously, I step my right foot firmly onto the earth. Something happens. My mind and foot are in concert. I step with my left foot, exhale, and "out" vibrates in my mind. My awareness of the unison strengthens. "Deep," "slow," does just that—my breath becomes full of life, and my body, the body that always wants to go faster in these mindfulness walks, instead transforms into a languid, deliberate shape. "Calm" and "ease" permeates the whole of it, as a smile lightens my face and tension releases out of my body. In just a few moments, wonder has filled my whole being.

In the present moment.

I now see Vanna, my negative seed trigger, across the green field, and for a moment I am pulled out of my wonderful ease. The sight of her agitates the memory of being shamelessly ridiculed for simply helping her communicate with a French Sister. I still don't understand what happened. But there she is again, amongst my friends, the trees. I had tried to clear the air with Vanna once before, but I had left in exasperation. I could only see her as arrogant and firmly unapologetic.

My Irish friend Aidan now comes to mind. I remember our walk together, and the difficulties he had had with his wife. I think of Aidan's astounding ability to embrace his negative emotions with compassion and understanding, immediately, as soon as they surfaced. Aidan's deep looking had fostered compassion within, and also toward his wife. Lucid with insight, Aidan knew what to do, how to wisely relate to his difficult feelings and relationships.

I look purposely over toward Vanna. Resentment is instantly there. I let that emotion stay. I breathe and embrace that awful feeling with a kind of awareness. I do not push it away. And I start to have what I would describe as an enhanced perception of my resentment. I understand *why* I feel disturbed by Vanna. No one likes to be ridiculed, and she had ridiculed me. I fully accept this. In the next moment, a compassionate feeling for my self arises, and I soften. I am walking through the whole of it, on the wet grass with the happy nuns. I am embracing and wrapping my mindfulness around my difficult emotions. More steps. More breaths. More understanding. The tension breaks down—in my mind and then in my body. More steps. More breaths. More light. Compassion flows for my self. And then, without difficulty, that tenderness expands outwards. I wonder what kind of life Vanna has had. My compassion turns toward her and moves out from me, like two long arms of light reaching across the field to envelope darkness. And then I know what to do.

> If we could read the secret history of our enemies, we should find in each man's life sorrow and suffering enough to disarm all hostility.
>
> —HENRY WADSWORTH LONGFELLOW

My eyes are back on Thây's calm, powerful aura as he walks toward the residence of New Hamlet. Sureness, grace, and intelligent humility are rays of brilliance emanating from his moving body. The monk pauses to gaze at a tree. I wonder what's in his mind, what he sees in the tree.

I have heard other pilgrims talk of various transcendent experiences they have had involving Thây. One woman relayed a story of a time when for a few moments she was alone with Thây in the kitchen as he walked through that room. That would have been a highly unusual occurrence. The blessed pilgrim had then become the receiver of a personal reverent bow from the transcendent monk, causing her to nearly faint with elation.

I haven't told anyone about the monk and me transforming into our five year-old selves until I write this now. I have met my hermit.

➣ Day 37 ➢

Work:
The Lawyer Who Became a Nun

*Pray as though everything depended on God. Work as
though everything depended on you.*

—SAINT AUGUSTINE

The evening meal has just finished and I am now sitting in the front room of New Hamlet with Sister
Pine. The American nun is much taller than every one
of the other Sisters here, and her presence is as strong as
her height. A confident and intelligent air surrounds her.
When I first laid eyes on Sister Pine, whose name implic-
itly means Enduring Freshness, I was equally drawn to
and intimidated by her until I saw that her sureness carried with it a wise humility and grace. Sister Pine is not
like the demure monastics. She looks utterly fearless. As
it turns out, this Plum Village nun with the everlasting
name, who is "green even in winter," used to be an animal rights lawyer back in the U.S. I imagine that she was
just as fair in the real world as she is living in her beloved
community of fellow Buddhists. I sit here in admiration

of the lawyer-turned-Buddhist, curious about what drew this captivating nun to such a different life, in a country far away from her homeland. I ask Sister Pine to tell me her story. She answers with no hesitation.

"Becoming a nun ultimately helps the world even more than being a good lawyer."

Sister Pine had been a lay-practitioner with Thich Nhat Hanh for many years before her ordainment. During that time, she had realized her greatest happiness, and had eventually come back to take her vows and live at Plum Village full time. "But don't you miss your work?" I ask. "You were doing such good things in the world." She easily replies that she doesn't miss her previous occupation and enjoys seeing the many people transformed by her direct efforts as a nun. "But don't you miss having a partner?" I press. She had been married, and had had a partner up until a few years before her ordainment. I ask her if she misses having an intimate loved one in her life. She again thoughtfully informs me that now she has time to generate unconditional love for all beings. I study her face. I am convinced.

> A nun lives in the fires of the spirit.
> —ANNIE DILLARD, HOLY THE FIRM

She makes it sound so very simple, but I know it's not easy. The Sisters of this French monastery are completely devoted to their work and practice. And there are many hours of spiritual practice and necessary tasks to attend to each day. Have I mentioned their lack of any real privacy? All sorts of people regularly come and go from the monastery—the nun's home—and their arms always stretch wide open to embrace these visitors. I try to imagine having a constant rotation of guests in my home. I am unable to picture it. The Sisters sleep in shared rooms, on wooden beds without mattresses, and there's not a bathtub in sight. And then, of course, there's the celibacy thing.

I tell Sister Pine she is courageous. She tells me she is lucky.

✼

At the end of my very first Vipassana Buddhist meditation retreat in the year 2000, I had a conversation with a young man who had unwittingly attended this same course at the insistence of his girlfriend. At that time, after the ten-day program had finished, up in the gorgeous Himalayan Mountains, my every cell was jumping with happiness. In my state of elation, I had floated over to this dark, curly-haired twenty-something guy to ask how he was feeling, thinking, of course, that he would be just as high as me. He wasn't. I'll never forget his answer. My fellow meditator looked directly at me and said that he felt as if his mind was a huge garbage bin full of foul, rotting filth, and that the act of meditating had opened the lid on the squalid mess that was his mind. As this new meditator had continued to practice, he began to dump the trash, but, "with only the tiniest of toothpicks for a tool," he told me.

Upon hearing my fellow voyager's account, I snapped out of my post-meditation bliss to see a face full of mental anguish. This young man was an engineer of rifles, guns, and ammunition of all sorts, and thoroughly enjoyed his profession. He said that during times of boredom throughout the meditations, he would distract himself by creating new weapons designs in his head. A few days into the retreat, there had been an evening discourse on the Buddhist tenet of Right Work—a teaching stipulating that one's work should positively support living beings, community, and the environment. Upon hearing about the teachings, the young man had become despondent and depressed. It had been the first time this man had looked deeply into the destructive nature of his profession, and it had shocked him. At the same time, however, the meditation practice had been steadily strengthening him, and by the end of the course, my fellow meditator had told me that he imagined a new beginning for himself—a future without guns, and one in which he could not only stop destruction, but also contribute to the well-being of all life.

※ ※

As I continue to visit with Sister Pine in a cozy nook in the front room of New Hamlet, the two of us cradling mugs of hot ginger tea, I am reminded of the Buddhist principle of Right Work and responsibility. The American nun has the kind of mind that I love. It is sharp, compassionate, and active, with many ideas and possible solutions to difficult problems. I wonder now if she might have some advice for a family member of mine who is having real trouble. She does, in fact, offer many innovative solutions to my query.

We sit in silence. I ponder the fact that some people move from good work to another kind of good work— the animal rights lawyer becomes a nun. I remember that there's the kind of person who wakes up to the destructive impact of their work on the world and decides to change—the weapons engineer discovers the transformative powers of meditation in India. In the year 2000, on top of a very high and sacred mountain, a transformed man told me that a Buddhist meditation course in the Himalayas had completely changed his life. The arms builder said, all those years ago, that he planned to quit his work—stop altogether. The weapons engineer turned Buddhist meditator had developed a new kind of respect and reverence for all the living beings of the world. Hallelujah.

The bad things, don't do them.
The good things, try to do them.
Try to purify, subdue your own mind.
That is the teaching of all buddhas.
—TRANSLATION FROM THE CHINESE DHAMMAPADA,
FROM THE ART OF POWER BY THICH NHAT HANH

Back at the monastery, earlier today, Thây had asked all of us the following question, "What are you doing?" He then told us that this simple question is the *only* question we need to ask ourselves in order to ensure that we are deeply engaged with our lives.

I say goodnight to Sister Pine and walk back to the dining hall, refill my cup with ginger tea, and sit by the fireplace. I reflect upon Thây's morning talk.

As you write, know that you are writing, and think of the people that will be helped from your writing. Hope that those who read your work will have happier lives. This is the same with all jobs. Do the job in mindfulness, with love for all people. Do this by asking yourself, "What am I doing?" Then you can produce a miracle.

At the end of the day, as I head up the stairs to my bedroom, my fondness grows for the Sister of Enduring Freshness, the former animal rights lawyer who wanted to do even *more* good in the world, and so became a nun. And I remember the gun-maker from the Himalayas, my fellow novice meditator, whom I had met all those years ago, and think, "Whatever he is doing now, there's one fewer bright mind in the world figuring out the latest in rifles."

212

⌐ Day 38 ⌐

Gratitude:
What a Single Pomegranate
Seed Taught Me

*Let us rise up and be thankful, for if we didn't learn a lot
today, at least we learned a little, and if we didn't learn a
little, at least we didn't get sick, and if we got sick at least
we didn't die; so, let us all be thankful.*

—THE BUDDHA

If you have never experienced a formal lunch at a monastery, you have no idea what it means to be truly
patient.

All common meals take place in the dining hall,
whereas formal lunches are eaten in the Buddha Hall. The
formal lunch goes like this: everyone lines up at the food
table, as usual, in the regular dining area, but instead of
"first come, first served," the senior monks and nuns go to
the front, followed by the younger monastics, followed by
the lay-practitioners. One by one, each person puts some
food in their bowl and then makes their way silently to the

Buddha Hall. Once in the room, monks and men sit on one side, and nuns and women on the other. The sexes are reverently divided in this Buddhist ritual. Both groups face in toward the center of the hall.

Because today is a formal day of mindfulness, I am now walking silently with my bowl of food toward the Buddha Hall of Upper Hamlet. The hall is about half full when I arrive and take my seat on the female side. You could hear a pin drop. Across from me I see several monks sitting patiently in neat rows on blue cushions, cross-legged, straight-backed and serene, their earth-colored robes draped gracefully around their knees. The rest of us look a little awkward, somehow. "Robes are much easier to manage than clothes," I decide. And shaved heads always look so clean—no messy hair falling on shoulders. Monastic bowls sit just as reverently before these peaceful creatures. Upon being ordained, monks are given a monk bowl to be used from that point on for their meals. This special bowl also carries a spiritual symbolism—it represents the monk's willingness to accept whatever is put in their bowl, physical or spiritual. Monks are said to deeply explore the personal relevance of this symbol of acceptance, the monk's bowl. In some Buddhist traditions, through their training, monks see their bowl as The Treasure House of the Eye of the True Teaching which is the Wondrous Heart of Nirvana. I have never heard of a more beautiful description for a simple food container.

Here in the hall where the valor of the Buddha reigns, with my Treasure House on my lap, I am knee to knee with my female neighbors, waiting for everyone else to arrive. There are several hundred of us gathered at Plum Village, so it will easily take another forty minutes before all are seated. During the wait, I alternate between gazing at the many Buddha-like faces across from me, and closing my eyes to focus on my breath.

Today in the monastery, I am learning the art of mindful eating, which works on one's capacity to endure waiting, to put it mildly. There's not a peep in the hall. I see the Willem Dafoe lookalike monk sitting reverently, sharp and clear-looking as always. I cast my gaze along the first row of senior monks. They sit with confidence, like the resilient Buddhas they've become. In the next row sit monks of lesser years, exuding varying degrees of sureness. The playful adolescent monks relax in the last rows and they look as if they've just come from a soccer match (and they very well could have). One by one, the familiar faces of my male friends find their seats alongside the monks. I steal glances at all of them, as outright looking would not be appropriate. My favorite pilgrim and master cook Stuart the Scot enters, followed by Gustavo—a more gentle and loving man you will never meet. I have come to love Gustavo like a perfect brother. A pang of guilt jabs at me. While I had been avoiding the lay-friends gathering on that infamous day of conspiring to hide my fellow pilgrim Rita from the unsuspecting monks, my thoughtful surrogate brother had been terribly worried that I might be sick or that I'd left the monastery. When Gustavo told me of his concern later, I became doubly ashamed at my thoughtless behavior. Next up, the sweet but complex Newfoundlander rolls in, the singer of Celtic ditties, from my day of cooking with the boys. Several other men follow, all of whom evoke a particular feeling or thought within me.

My Treasure House is still on my lap. My female neighbors are not in my view, and I can't keep staring at the monks and men and imagining their histories, so instead I reflect on this everyday act of consuming food. I turn my focus toward the sound and sensation of my breathing and silently repeat the mantra, "Breathing in, I know I am breathing in. Breathing out, I know I am breathing out." The directed attention calms my swirling thoughts. It doesn't take long to alter one's state through mantra and breath focus, but sometimes I am surprised at how quickly it works. I open my eyes and look into the sacred food within this divinely symbolic bowl. A multitude of brilliant colors pop immediately— the food is shining. But what strikes me the most are the stunning crimson-drenched pomegranate seeds. It seems as if they are talking to me: "Look at us, how gorgeous we are." I am absorbed in the beauty of simple red seeds. Indescribable joy moves within.

In this state of immersion, I have gone Home to myself. Thây reminds us regularly that "thinking may cause us to lose ourselves." Through mindful breathing, we unify the body and mind and establish ourselves in the here and now. Secured in the present moment is the only way to see what is truly there. That is why I am able to see the pomegranate seed today. In this morning's talk, Thây had elaborated on the use of this practice to stabilize ourselves in all situations, particularly difficult ones. If, for example, we feel lost because of some turbulent event or emotion, we should "close the six sense doors" of our eyes, ears, nose, tongue, body, and mind in order to become calm and gain clarity. The monk described it like a house with several windows and doors; if we open all of them when there are strong winds, the wind will blow everything about. "Going Home is like shutting the windows and doors, so that the wind won't penetrate. And then, once we feel safe, we may want to carefully open one window to see what's going on out there."

In the teachings of Islam, it is said that the heart is enlightened for forty days with the eating of a pomegranate.

Nhat Hanh means "one action at one time." Graced with this deceptively simple name from his teacher, Thich Nhat Hanh worked to master this difficult focus throughout his life. Now, here, I am about to do one thing at one time, with as much laser focus as I can manage. This is what Thây has been trying to teach us, day after day.

Mindfulness. What are you doing? Engage fully. What is there? What is the reality of the moment? These pomegranate seeds I am about to mindfully ingest have just been truly *seen* by me for the second time in my life, even though I have for many years loved and eaten this luscious fruit. I have a childhood memory of living in Windsor, Ontario as an eight-year-old, intensely delighted upon trying the exotic pomegranate for the first time. The memory now blends into this moment here, as I sit in wonder at the miracle that is a pomegranate. All the elements of the world created this wondrous fruit. The earth, water, sun, air, and various minerals all contributed to the birth of the pomegranate, not to mention the farmers and grocery store clerks. The whole cosmos is in the pomegranate. In this vital moment of knowing, I see the real pomegranate.

A pomegranate is not a pomegranate. That is why it is a real pomegranate.

⚜

Thây has uttered this following piece of wisdom countless times: "You must recognize what is right in front of you now." And when you do, you will be thankful. Buddhist gratitude involves an awareness of thanks toward our parents, for giving us our body; our teachers, for giving us guidance; and our friends, for supporting us. Our thanks should ultimately embrace all living beings. We must also revere the sky, as it protects us like an umbrella; and the earth, for it supports us. When we understand that without the earth, we cannot stand, we develop the insight of gratitude toward our terrain and become naturally thankful for everything surrounding us.

After my pomegranate lunch today I meet Chaya, a thirty-something Jewish Israeli who has a home on the Gaza Strip. She is a visitor here, like me, but will stay for just one week. This afternoon, our new pilgrim joins the group to discuss Thich Nhat Hanh's Dharma talk from this morning. There are about ten of us outside in the sunny garden of Upper Hamlet, sitting on a circle of chairs, as the grass is damp today. Chaya follows the procedure to announce that she is about to speak by pressing her hands together in prayer pose at her heart and bowing slightly. Appearances don't necessarily reveal life history. Chaya begins to reflect aloud on what brought her to Plum Village. She tells everybody in the discussion group that a childhood of relentless physical abuse had launched her search for peace. I listen now to Chaya talk matter-of-factly about the harrowing abuse she had suffered throughout her life. There is no lingering resentment in her voice. Upon hearing Chaya's tragic tale, I am graced with a deep appreciation for the true love and support of my parents while they were alive. Even in their deaths, their love continues to live on within me.

Today, I crossed the finish line of the marathon that is a formal lunch in the Zen Buddhist tradition. It is a worthy feat. And I am grateful. May we all be grateful.

☞ Day 39 ☜

Prayer:
The Day the Monks Sang

where I does not exist, nor you,
so close that your hand on my chest is my hand,
so close that your eyes close as I fall asleep.

— PABLO NERUDA

This thirty-ninth morning, I have written a prayer on a small piece of yellow paper and placed it in the large bell jar that sits at the front of the Buddha Hall. On previous days I have heard Thây read these prayers of the pilgrims aloud.

Some days ago, the Willem Dafoe lookalike monk let me in on a little secret. He said that Thây often teaches with his eyes. That is, he directs his gaze toward various people, in synchrony with the words that specific person needs to hear. My friend and Brother went on to give me several miraculous examples of his experience with this.

Thây strikes a match. He lifts the flame and asks, "Has this flame always been here?" Then he takes a candle and lights the wick with the flame from the match and asks,

219

"Is this second flame of the candle, the same as the first flame of the match?" Thây blows out the first flame. The Zen master's deep, black eyes dive into mine. "Is the first flame *in* the second flame?"

I close my eyes. The golden image stays, and I feel my mother, the first flame, within me, the second flame. The first flame has not died. An image of my mother's handwriting comes into my mind. I have a written note by my mother, which I found in her wallet after she died. That note is in my own wallet now.

> Do not stand by my grave and cry. I am not
> there. I did not die.
>
> —MARY FRYE

I do not cry. My mother is here. My mother did not die. I fold my hands together—my mother's hands entwine. Our eyes look into our hands in my lap. The shape of the nails on our fingers are the same smooth ovals. Long fingers on dancer's hands. My hand lifts to touch my cheek. It is the hand of my mother. And this hand is also on my mother's gentle face. I bring my hand from her face and our hands entwine on my lap. These hands touch my past. These hands live in my present. These hands create my future. My hands are my mother's hands. My mother's hands are mine.

Thây speaks again. "The creature contains the creator. The daughter contains the mother. You cannot separate them."

When certain conditions come together, we manifest. The flame manifested because Thây struck the match, causing it to catch fire. The flame went out because conditions changed—Thây blew on the flame. After he had blown the flame out he said, "The one who has died in fact has not died. They have simply grown into a form that may be unfamiliar to you." This is not an abstract idea. It is a reality. Then, Thây asked all of us where our five-year-old selves had gone. He answered that question by saying that she or he had simply grown into a woman or a man.

Your five-year-old self has continued on to become your adult self now. Your five-year-old self is not the same as your adult self, but she is not different either. The Buddha taught: "Neither the same, nor different." Thây then said: "We have to transcend sameness and otherness. If you can speak to your five-year-old self, you can also communicate with the one you think has died. She is always there. You can always communicate with her," The monk has spoken.

Thây left us with this reminder: "Your nature is no birth, no death. The person you think has died is also of the nature of no birth, no death. You are free from being and non-being."

<hr>

It's the end of the day and Thây gracefully reaches into the bowl containing the prayers of the pilgrims. From this pool of hope, the Zen master plucks out my yellow note and reads it aloud. "Dear Thây, Dear Sangha, please send your healing energy to my brother, Iain, who for many years has suffered from terrible back pain due to herniated discs. Many thanks, Mary." Hearing my words in Thây's voice sparks me awake.

Like the conductor of some divine orchestra, Thây lifts his hand and a multitude of obedient monks in brown robes begin chanting. The particular sutra is a recitation of the names of five Bodhisattvas—beings whose essence is enlightenment. This chant is said to call on these help- ful beings so that one's prayers may be heard.

Blending in with the voices, Thây gracefully invites a large bell to sound, as an equally reverent monk strikes a smaller wooden bell. Together the bells create a mesmerizing beat to accompany the chanting monks and nuns. To me, here and now, this sound vibration carries enormous, healing power. And it is a rising and glorious sound.

Prayers and mantras alter one's consciousness. Brain chemistry changes, emotions balance, even the immune system is enhanced. And then there's the repetitive nature of chanting and its vibratory effect on one's whole being. In our world, we live in a virtual ocean of energetic vibrations. Even inanimate objects are nothing but a mass of vibrations. The chair you are sitting on is vibrating. This book is vibrating. You are vibrating. I am vibrating. The monk in front of me is vibrating. As the monk chants, he both creates and becomes a sacred vibration, and the sounds vibrate within me. An intelligent presence surrounds it all.

Mantra and prayer have a mysterious power that cannot be logically explained.

Thây sits in an easy, cross-legged posture, with a spine that appears much straighter and younger than his eighty-four years. The Zen master's eyes are closed. With one expert hand he plays the bell; with the other he touches his thumb tip to alternate fingertips. For a moment I wonder exactly what he is doing with this sound current, because magic is happening. I close my eyes and the power hits me. It strikes me exactly in my heart, causing quiet tears to stream down my cheeks. I am visualizing Iain, who had been so completely devoted to our ailing father, and I am wishing that my brother be freed from his excruciating back pain.

As I listen to this immaculate Bodhisaatva choir, I again feel the power of community. These Brothers and Sisters love each other, and they draw support and strength from their communal living. I hear it inside of their chanting voices. Before every mantra, the Plum Village Sangha and visiting pilgrims are asked to chant as one body—to unify and actualize the power in the collective. "Our consciousness is fed with other consciousnesses." As Thây spoke, I was reminded of this reality.

The way we make decisions, our likes and dislikes, all depend on the collective way of seeing things. At one point, near the beginning of my pilgrimage, Thây had given an example of how someone may not see some thing as beautiful, like a painting for example, but if many others think that work of art is beautiful, then slowly that person may come to accept beauty there as well, whether or not that is true. This is simply because the individual consciousness is made up of the collective, and we are all influenced by the collective ways of seeing and thinking. Thây talks of the importance of surrounding ourselves with people who emit loving kindness, understanding, and compassion, because we are influenced by the collective consciousness all the time.

A lovely Dutch pilgrim recently told me that upon her return to Amsterdam, she would set about finding mindful housemates with which to share her dwelling. Here at the monastery, the pilgrim understood her loneliness and the importance of immersing herself in a loving community.

<hr />

The last of the resounding notes of the sutra have left the air full of a spirit-boosting pizzazz. Everyone in the hall appears enlivened. Both of my loving brothers now come to mind. I see my father in my brothers. Our father is in the shape of their hands, the kindness of their hearts, and the values that they live. I simply have to look at my brothers to see that my father is alive. That is the miracle of prayer.

⊱ Day 40 ⊰

Love:
Floating on a Lotus Leaf

It is love alone that gives worth to all things.

—SAINT TERESA OF AVILA

When I was eleven years old, I played Mary in the Nativity play at the Presbyterian Church of my best friend's minister father. I had been raised Roman Catholic, but regularly went to Presbyterian Sunday school to hang out with my best friend, Jean. We did everything together. My mother would drop me by the Presbyterian Church after our family had attended Catholic mass together. My best friend, however, had not been permitted to attend Catholic mass with me. One day during Sunday school, a mother of one of the other children there, having heard a Catholic was wandering around the church basement with the minister's daughter, approached me and asked why I was at this Presbyterian church and not at my *own* Catholic church. Somehow I said, "God is in me, so I can go anywhere." The woman didn't say a word to me after that.

Many years later, I realized that my parents, with their inclusive, non-discriminating, and loving natures, had been responsible for my eleven-year-old views.

꧁ ꧂

It is Christmas Eve. The emptiness of the black country sky is filled with moonlight, and I am sitting in the big meditation hall at New Hamlet, listening to the monks sing "O Come, All Ye Faithful" as glimmering star ornaments hang from pine Christmas trees. The inclusive Thich Nhat Hanh has had his Buddhist monastery decorated with typically Christian fare. It is brilliant.

A fresh evergreen scent wafts from four Christmas trees erected in this Buddhist meditation hall—one to represent each Hamlet of Plum Village. Multi-colored lights brighten the doorways and windows behind them. Just one thing stands out amongst the traditional holiday fare. At the front, by the Buddha statue, there is a small boat crafted from bamboo wood and filled with stunning roses of various shades of pink. This is the only unusual Christmas decoration.

Thây glides toward the bamboo vessel, kneels down in front, examines it, and then turns and says to all gathered here, "Let me tell you what this is. This is the boat of understanding. It will bring you from the shore of suffering to the shore of love."

"There, he said it. This rose-filled boat is the image that will remind me to take refuge within my wise self," I realize. As I delve deep within, guided by the wise teachings of the Buddha, I will awaken understanding, and then wisdom will be roused—the key to liberation and a happier existence. The boat itself represents the teaching of the Buddha, and it carries within it the flowers—the understanding and insight—that will blossom within me as I follow that sacred guidance. I imagine myself now, among the delicate flowers in that boat of strength, rowing toward a pristine shore of love.

"My effort will protect me. No one else is there to paddle my boat. I have to do it." I take a photo of Thây beside the sacred vessel of pink roses.

When we have compassion toward ourselves, we are able to expand those benevolent feelings out toward others. "This boat carries understanding, which brings love. Without understanding it is not possible to love— your love is not *true love*. When we completely understand others, we carry ourselves to the shore of freedom, love, and happiness." The peaceful monk smiles.

And there it is again. All of us are interconnected. We are all in this together. The truth surges forth and takes on greater meaning. To love and understand the self is to love and understand the other. And to have true compassion and understanding of the self is the only way to equally revere the other. More of Thây's words touch me. "In one truth lie all truths. One thing embraces all others. This is because of inter-being. All truths are interconnected just as all things and all beings are linked in the world. Therefore, if you understand one truth, you will understand all truths."

On this, my fortieth day, the insight fills my being.

Thây continues to offer us his vision on love. He teaches that the beloved lives all around us. They are the trees, air, water, and land. "When we fully understand our need for fresh air, to keep us healthy and alive, we gain a deep love for this vital oxygen." Thich Nhat Hanh talks of being loved *by* the trees. Many people easily profess their love *for* trees, but how many times have you heard someone say that the trees love them?

At dinnertime, I walk over to the gigantic four-foot-tall pot of soup that I spent the day making with Sister Prune. I dip the ladle into the sea of multi-colored veggies, and happiness drenches me. I take a seat beside Stuart, my Scottish cooking friend and most excellent culinary master. We talk about the soup we are both joyfully spooning into our mouths. He says the medley of veggies is delicious. My heart warms. Stuart offers to give me a number of his best soup recipes to take back to Canada. I love being with Stuart. He is kind and genuine—a bona fide spirit. And I always hear my Scottish father in Stuart's rolling Edinburgh lilt.

The Christmas musical performances begin. A British monk glides a curved bow along the strings of a cello. I ask Stuart about this Brother. He says that the cello-playing monk used to be in the symphony in London. I instinctively say, "He should be playing in a concert hall so that people can enjoy his tremendous gift." Stuart's soft brown eyes meet mine as he quietly says, "Well, you're enjoying his music, aren't you?" I am stunned. Of course I am. Why do I think that it's any different? There are hundreds of people here in the hall enjoying this monk's expert musical gift.

Stuart then asks me about the "secret Santa" gifts. Earlier in the week, all of the monastics and visiting pilgrims pulled names out of a big jar. We were to anonymously give a gift to the person whose name we drew. I tell Stuart my "secret Santa" pick. Stuart knows the woman who will receive a present from me. He tells me that she is staying at Lower Hamlet, miles away from New Hamlet, my residence. Stuart reveals that my "secret Santa" pick is about to give birth, and so had to leave Plum Village before the Christmas celebration began. Her husband will be collecting his pregnant wife's gift. My mouth drops wide open. Unbeknownst to me, this pregnant pilgrim was at the monastery. There are hundreds of people in Plum Village spread across four hamlets, and I drew the name of the only pregnant woman here. My gift to her is a book that I had brought with me from Canada called *The Birth House*. I squeeze Stuart's knee so hard he yelps.

Christmas is a time to reflect on how to build a true family where everyone is rooted in everyone else. There is no distinction

227

between the lover and the loved. This is equanimity. Equanimity does not equal exclusiveness. Equanimity does not take sides. It does not discriminate. Equanimity equals inclusiveness.

The collective is made up of individual awakenings, and those awakenings are contagious. Therefore, one awake person may bring about the awakenings of others. It always begins with you—you are the one you must count on. Thây's wise words vibrate in the air.

And there it is. I enlighten and fortify my self by taking refuge within. I become a wise rock—a happy, wise, and solid rock. Only then, with more joy in my own life, will I be able to uplift others. I remember the words of Mother Teresa: "Let no one ever come to you without leaving better and happier. Be the living expression of God's kindness: kindness in your face, kindness in your eyes, kindness in your smile."

Walk toward joy, love and virtue. Give weight to your courage. Foster insight—wisdom will keep you sane and full of life. Share your unique gifts with the world. Surround yourself with those who encourage and support an elevated awareness. The power of the collective consciousness is not to be underestimated. We are, all of us, greatly influenced by our surroundings. Sage advice from Thich Nhat Hanh.

Going Home

We are going home in every moment—We are practically
⌣ *going home in every moment to mother earth, to God,*
to the ultimate dimension, to our true nature of no birth
no death. That is our true home. We have never left our
home.

—THICH NHAT HANH

I am standing outside with my suitcase on the steps of
New Hamlet. My forty-day pilgrimage has come to
completion. It is a golden sunny day for my departure
home. Before I leave, there is one more thing I must
do. As a final gesture of forgiveness, and in the spirit of
Beginning Anew, the Sister's practice for healing relationships, I have picked a purple wildflower for Vanna.
The upset from that day of the French translation in the
Buddha Hall has diminished. It has receded only because
I've been practicing embracing with understanding my
negative feelings toward my fellow pilgrim. It has worked.
Hearing the happy Irishman's tales of fostering mindfulness toward his own feelings of anger, triggered by his
difficult marriage, has strengthened my resolve. Aidan
had applied the Buddha's teachings to real life, and they
worked. That gave him clarity. In *Cultivating the Mind*

of Love, Thich Nhat Hanh reminds us of a power that is always available: "When you feel others trying to destroy you, if you touch the love in yourself, you will not be harmed."

Mindfulness is an essential life skill. Being aware of what is truly there in the moment is the only way to gain the kind of insight that will allow you to flourish and soar. And in those moments of knowing, past wounds are healed, afflictions vanish, emotions are honored and understood, compassion and love arise, relationships are saved, obsessions lose their grip, opportunities are recognized, and a deep, abiding security within the wise self reigns. There is an endless list of benefits.

Purple flower in hand, I scan the area for Vanna. All the pilgrims are milling about, but now, when I *want* to find Vanna, she is nowhere to be seen. My ride to the train station is patiently waiting. I scribble a few kind words on a note torn from my journal and wrap it around the wild-flower with a bit of string. I see Vanna's roommate nearby and ask her to give the flower to the American pilgrim. In an instant, I feel relief. And like petals opening on a lotus, joy begins to move within me. I don't know if my gesture will ease Vanna's negative feelings toward me. I hope so. I realize, though, that a genuine *mea culpa* is what's important, no matter what response it brings. Authentic kindness in and of itself brings relief, and this Buddhist flower-giving is brilliant. Turning a Western notion on its head by blessing your "enemies" with flowers—only the Buddhists would think of that. Flowers for everyone! This may be my new motto. I will need this Eastern skill back home. It will save me over and over, and it will enrich all of my relationships. You will see this too—it is a miracle.

I am going Home in every moment.

Sister Hanh Nghiêm is standing in the doorway of the majestic grey stone building of New Hamlet, her home. I approach the nun who has been adorned with the name "action," and bid farewell. We embrace—a hug that is

long and true—and say nothing. The next moment, I am in a silver-grey Renault on my way to the train station.

On the train to Bordeaux, another teaching from the sage comes to mind: "When you can produce a thought of reconciliation, a thought of compassion, this kind of thinking heals you and begins to heal the world. As a practitioner, you can produce this kind of thinking many times a day. If you can think like this, you will transform yourself and you will transform the world."

Thây's guidance will stay with me forever. I have understood how to take refuge within my wise self, how to foster compassion for the whole of my being. And, in going Home to myself, I am fully present for everyone. Compassion and love for all life comes from this deep Home within. I think now of this yearning for a true Home that had launched me on my pilgrimage to Plum Village—the quest for a strong, wise place to dwell, to transcend the pain and loneliness of losing my parents, and to skillfully navigate the turbulent waters of life.

I think back to the inaugural words of Thich Nhat Hanh: "In the stormy ocean of life, take refuge in your wise self." To be in the exquisite presence, depth of insight, and love of Thây is to touch freedom. I look out the train window at the rolling moss-green hills and wintry grapevines of the French countryside and make a silent vow to always remember.

I have never left my Home.

Acknowledgments

I am deeply thankful for the love and support of my brothers David Paterson and Iain Paterson and my sister-in-law Janice Gould-Paterson. My nephews Tobin and Devin and my niece Tara fill my life with joy.

It's true that a whole team of people is required to create a book. Everything is interconnected and interdependent. With that truth in mind, my thanks to Lorna Owen for early editorial assistance, Patrick Crean for his devoted friendship, valued reading, and ongoing advice, Ken McGoogan for excellent tips of the craft, Susan Swan and my wise fellow writers of Toronto; my wonderful agent Shaun Bradley for her abiding support, Samantha Haywood, and everyone at Transatlantic Literary Agency. A very special thanks to my editor Caroline Pincus for her enthusiasm and expertise, and to Rachel Leach, Susie Pitzen, Pat Rose, and everyone at Hampton Roads Publishing.

Thanks to all my great and generous friends at Lotus Yoga Centre in Toronto, especially Leea Litzgus, who took my suitcase back to Toronto from France; and Shauna MacDonald, for my writing retreat at her cottage. Thanks as well to Wagamama and Manic cafes.

My heartfelt thanks to the Buddha, Thich Nhat Hanh, Sister Pine, and all the monks and nuns of Plum Village—brilliant lotuses all of them. A salute to my fellow pilgrims. And finally, my deep thanks to you.

Resources

Books by Thich Nhat Hanh

Anger
The Art of Power
Buddha Mind, Buddha Body
Cultivating the Mind of Love
The Diamond That Cuts Through Illusion
The Heart of the Buddha's Teachings
The Heart of Understanding: Commentaries on the Prajna-
paramita Heart Sutra
no death, no fear
The World We Have

Other Resources

The Creation—An Appeal to Save Life on Earth, E.O.
Wilson
The Five Tibetans, Christopher S. Kilham
Giving, Bill Clinton
Holy the Firm, Annie Dillard
How Shakespeare Changed Everything, Stephen Marche
Joyful Wisdom, Yongey Mingyur Rinpoche
Path to Bliss, His Holiness The Dalai Lama
The Shambhala Sun
Tao Te Ching, Translation by Stephen Mitchell
The Tibetan Book of Living and Dying, Sogyal Rinpoche
The Vanishing Face of Gaia, James Lovelock

About the Author

Mary Paterson is the founder and director of Toronto's Lotus Yoga Centre. Certified in Kundalini and Hatha yoga, Mary also holds a Bachelor of Arts, and teaches internationally. She has been interviewed for numerous magazines and newspapers, including Elle Canada, The Toronto Star, and The Globe and Mail, and has regularly contributed celebrity health profiles to online journals. Mary is often invited by a variety of companies to teach and speak about the transformational powers of yoga and meditation. Trained in classical ballet, Mary also performed professionally in theatre and film. She has travelled throughout India and now lives in Toronto, Canada.

Visit Mary at *www.lotusyogacentre.com*.

About Thich Nhat Hanh and Plum Village

The Venerable Thich Nhat Hanh is a Vietnamese Buddhist monk, poet, scholar, and peace activist. His life-long efforts to generate peace moved Martin Luther King, Jr. to nominate him for the Nobel Peace Prize in 1967. Thich Nhat Hanh is the founder of the Van Hanh Buddhist University in Saigon, the School for Youths of Social Services in Vietnam, and the Unified Buddhist Church in France. Plum Village is Thich Nhat Hanh's monastery for monks and nuns in the Aquitane region of France. It is also a mindfulness practice centre for lay-people. The year 2012 marks the thirtieth anniversary of Plum Village.

For further information about Plum Village and Thich Nhat Hanh, please visit *www.plumvillage.org*.

Hampton Roads Publishing Company
. . . for the evolving human spirit

Hampton Roads Publishing Company
publishes books on a variety of subjects,
including spirituality, health,
and other related topics.

For a copy of our latest trade catalog,
call (978) 465-0504 or visit our distributor's website at
www.redwheelweiser.com.
You can also sign up for our newsletter and special
offers by going to *www.redwheelweiser.com/newsletter/*.